American Revolution 1775–8

British Light Infantryman
VERSUS
Patriot Rifleman

COMBAT

Robbie MacNiven

Illustrated by Marco Capparoni

OSPREY PUBLISHING

Bloomsbury Publishing Plc

Kemp House, Chawley Park, Cumnor Hill, Oxford OX2 9PH, UK

29 Earlsfort Terrace, Dublin 2, Ireland

1385 Broadway, 5th Floor, New York, NY 10018, USA

E-mail: info@ospreypublishing.com

www.ospreypublishing.com

OSPREY is a trademark of Osprey Publishing Ltd

First published in Great Britain in 2023

A catalog record for this book is available from the British Library.

ISBN: PB 9781472857934; eBook 9781472857965;
ePDF 9781472857958; XML 9781472857941

23 24 25 26 27   10 9 8 7 6 5 4 3 2 1

Maps by www.bounford.com

Index by Rob Munro

Typeset by PDQ Digital Media Solutions, Bungay, UK

Printed and bound in India by Replika Press Private Ltd.

FSC MIX
Paper from responsible sources
FSC® C016779
www.fsc.org

Osprey Publishing supports the Woodland Trust, the UK's leading woodland conservation charity.

To find out more about our authors and books visit **www.ospreypublishing.com**. Here you will find extracts, author interviews, details of forthcoming events and the option to sign up for our newsletter.

Artist's note

Readers may care to note that the original paintings from which the color plates in this book were prepared are available for private sale. All reproduction copyright whatsoever is retained by the publishers. All inquiries should be addressed to:

marcocapparoni.com

The publishers regret that they can enter into no correspondence upon this matter.

CONTENTS

Introduction

Fighting in North America during the 18th century necessitated changes from the standard European model of combat. With more forested, broken or rugged terrain, armies came to rely on soldiers capable of fighting individually or in small groups. Ideal combatants were physically fit, good shots, and able to act independent of the higher chain of command. Regular linear warfare, while still practiced (and still decisive), was supplemented by these more irregular styles.

A typical Patriot rifleman of the American Revolutionary War period. His primary equipment consisted of a rifle, a powder horn, a bag with shot and patches, and a hunting knife. He was clad in a loose-fitting hunting shirt of the style that was popular on the frontier, and generally wore a broad-brimmed hat. (Stock Montage/Getty Images)

Even prior to the American Revolutionary War (1775–83), riflemen possessed a notable reputation in both the colonies and Britain. Rifled weaponry, while far from ubiquitous, was popular in America, especially on the frontiers, and its use transferred from hunting to war. At the start of the American Revolutionary War rifle-armed companies were the first units raised for the newly created Continental Army, but militiamen and partisans also made use of rifled weapons, which were usually employed in conjunction with irregular warfare. Patriot leaders initially placed great stock in the usefulness of the rifle, with some even believing it would be a decisive factor in winning the war.

The colonial predilection for the use of rifles and woodland fighting was well-known in Britain, as was the nature of the North American terrain itself. Even before the outbreak of hostilities, the British Army was making changes in an effort to prepare itself for a war in the Thirteen Colonies. Most significantly, light-infantry companies, which had been used to great effect

OPPOSITE
This print depicts Patriot forces engaging British troops at the battle of Lexington on April 19, 1775, in the first engagement of the American Revolutionary War. Patriot militia fought as skirmishers, ambushing the British column from woods, walls, and houses bordering the roadside. To counter this, the British deployed both the light infantry and grenadiers as skirmishers in their own right, chasing off militia or setting small, localized ambushes for them. (Stock Montage/Getty Images)

The Retreat

From Concord to Lexington of the Army of Wild Irish Asses Defeated by the Brave American Militia

Wr Deacon Mr Loeings Mr Mulikens Mr Bonds Houses and Barn all Plunder'd and Burnt on April 19th
A according to Act June 12 1775

The battle of Lexington, shown here in a contemporary illustration, was a stern test for the British light infantry. Unused to operating in battalions together, they were subjected to a daylong fighting retreat that nearly – but didn't quite – break the cohesion of the column of regulars. This propaganda piece depicts the British as "Wild Irish Asses" being driven off by brave American militia, who at this early stage of the war still fight under the Union Flag, in defense of what they saw as their English rights. While much of the image is fantastical, British light infantry and grenadiers did pillage and torch homesteads as the column's discipline unraveled throughout the retreat. (Fotosearch/Getty Images)

in America during the French and Indian War (1754–63) and in Europe during the Seven Years' War (1756–63), were reintroduced in 1771–72. British light infantrymen were among the most experienced soldiers in a given regiment, and were expected to be able to engage and defeat the Patriots in their "preferred style of fighting" – skirmishing in the woods. After the start of the American Revolutionary War the light companies quickly established a reputation as elite troops. The British also instituted the creation of the Army's first field service rifle, the Pattern 1776, to help redress the perceived imbalance in ranged combat.

On June 14, 1775, Congress authorized the raising of ten companies of riflemen as part of the ongoing creation and development of the Continental Army. Two of these rifle companies were to be recruited in Maryland, two in Virginia, and six in Pennsylvania, though efforts went so well in that last state that the number was raised to nine, forming an entire rifle regiment. These 13 rifle companies represented the initial core of rifle-armed Patriot troops, with more such companies being raised in the following year. Ultimately, rifle companies were included in many of the new Continental Army regiments, and there were also rifle-armed troops in the State and militia forces fighting for Congress. The rifle as a weapon therefore saw extensive service throughout the American Revolutionary War.

During the Seven Years' War it became common for the British Army to brigade the "flank" (light and grenadier) companies from standing regiments together to form composite battalions composed entirely of that troop type. Lieutenant-General William Howe, who would go on to serve as commander-in-chief of British land forces in North America from October 1775 through May 1778, commanded one of these light-infantry battalions during the Seven Years' War, and reintroduced the practice during the American Revolutionary War. In 1776, prior to the commencement of the campaign to capture New York in August, the light-infantry companies from over 30 line regiments were detached from their parent units and formed into three battalions for service together. While depriving the line regiments of some of

This illustration depicts a British light infantryman serving during the Seven Years' War, a conflict known in North America as the French and Indian War. The details – from the cap to the belly cartridge box, the black shoulder strap, the half-gaiters, the short jacket with shoulder wings, and the musket with fixed bayonet – are also characteristic of the British light infantry of the American Revolutionary War. (Anne S.K. Brown Military Collection, Brown University Library

MAP KEY

1   August 27, 1776: Crown Forces move from Staten Island to Long Island and defeat Patriot forces there, leading to a Patriot withdrawal to Manhattan.

2   September 15, 1776: A British landing is completed at Kip's Bay in an attempt to cut off Patriot troops in New York city.

3   September 15, 1776: Patriot forces escape before the British encirclement is complete. They begin to dig in farther north on Manhattan, at Harlem Heights.

4   September 16, 1776: A skirmish between pickets develops into the battle of Harlem Heights.

5   July 6, 1777: Crown Forces capture Fort Ticonderoga as part of their attempt to capture the length of the Hudson River and cut off New England.

6   July 7, 1777: The British attack and disperse the rear guard of Patriot forces withdrawing from Ticonderoga during the battle of Hubbardton.

7   August 16, 1777: A detachment of Hessians and Loyalists on a foraging expedition, separate from the main British army, is destroyed by Patriot forces at Bennington.

8   September 19, 1777: The British advance south along the bank of the Hudson River halts before entrenched Patriot forces at Bemis Heights. The Patriots advance from their lines, triggering the battle of Freeman's Farm.

9   May 12, 1780: Crown Forces capture Charleston, South Carolina.

10   August 1, 1780: Colonel Thomas Sumter's Patriot partisans launch an attack on the British outpost at Rocky Mount. The attack is repulsed.

11   August 1, 1780: In an attempt at diverting British attention, Sumter's subordinate, Major W.R. Davie, attacks the neighboring British outpost at Hanging Rock. The attack is successful, though the British maintain control of the outpost. Sumter decides to focus his forces in an attempt to capture Hanging Rock.

their best soldiers, this reorganization did ensure that British commanders had a cadre of elite battalions at their disposal, and these formations were heavily employed most often as part of an advance corps that was expected to conduct the heaviest fighting. The method of organizing composite battalions was repeated in different theaters throughout the American Revolutionary War, from Major-General John Burgoyne's Canadian expedition to the Loyalist Provincial Corps of light infantry that ended up operating in the South.

Patriot forces took similar measures. As well as forming light-infantry companies and battalions on a seasonal or campaign basis, Major General George Washington, commander-in-chief of the Continental Army, authorized the creation of rifle units drawn from the best marksmen and most able volunteers in the Continental Army regiments. The most famous of these units was formed in 1776, under the command of Colonel Daniel Morgan. They saw service in New Jersey in 1776–77 and played an important role at Saratoga before Morgan was deployed to the South, where Continental officers such as Colonel Thomas Sumter and Lieutenant Colonel Francis Marion commanded partisan units that made use of riflemen.

Throughout the American Revolutionary War both British light infantry and Patriot riflemen came to be considered among the best troops on either side. Their reputation among allies and the fear they provoked in the enemy was frequently noted. While riflemen tended to proliferate among Continental Army forces, however, light infantry were typically in short supply for Crown commanders. Because of this direct, prolonged combat during large-scale engagements between riflemen and light infantry was a rare occurrence – but when it did occur, the results were often desperate and deadly.

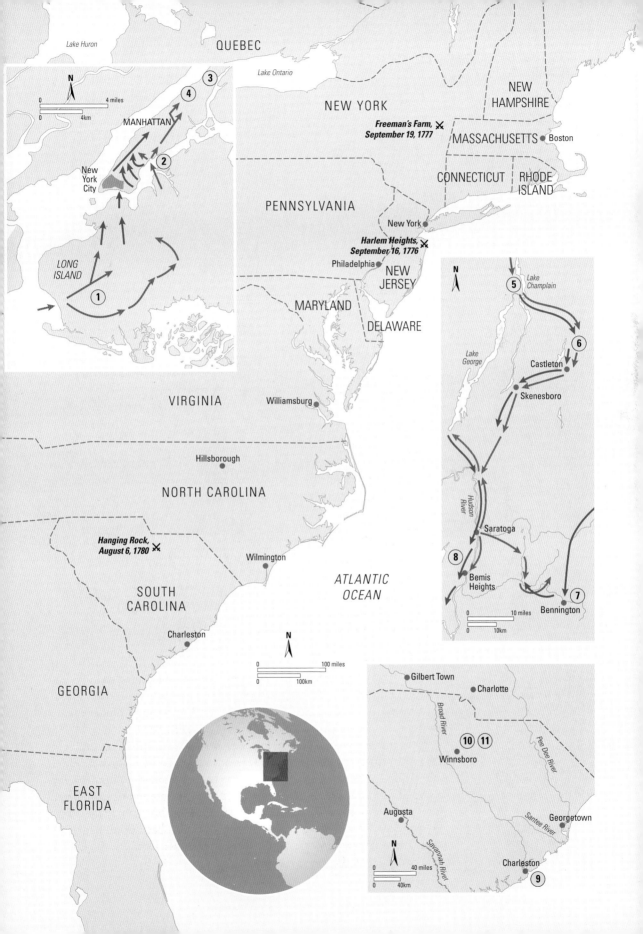

QUEBEC

Lake Huron

Lake Ontario

NEW YORK

NEW HAMPSHIRE

MASSACHUSETTS
Boston

*Freeman's Farm,
September 19, 1777*

CONNECTICUT | RHODE ISLAND

PENNSYLVANIA

New York

*Harlem Heights,
September 16, 1776*

Philadelphia

NEW JERSEY

MARYLAND

DELAWARE

VIRGINIA

Williamsburg

Hillsborough

NORTH CAROLINA

*Hanging Rock,
August 6, 1780*

Wilmington

SOUTH CAROLINA

Charleston

ATLANTIC OCEAN

GEORGIA

EAST FLORIDA

0   100 miles
0   100km

N

MANHATTAN

New York City

LONG ISLAND

0   4 miles
0   4km

N

③ ④ ② ①

Lake Champlain

⑤ ⑥

Castleton

Skenesboro

Lake George

Hudson River

Saratoga

⑧ Bemis Heights

Bennington ⑦

0   10 miles
0   10km

N

Gilbert Town

Charlotte

Broad River

Pee Dee River

⑩ ⑪

Winnsboro

Augusta

Santee River

Georgetown

Savannah River

Charleston

⑨

0   40 miles
0   40km

N

The Opposing Sides

FIREPOWER

Patriot

Rifled barrels allowed for greater accuracy, with the weapons being effective at 200yd and still capable of hitting targets at 400yd. Accounts of the accuracy of American riflemen abounded, especially at the start of the American Revolutionary War. Rifle companies put on displays of marksmanship that awed onlookers. One surgeon noted that

> these men are remarkable for the accuracy of their aim, striking a mark with great certainty at two hundred yards distance. At a review, a company of them, while in a quick advance, fired their balls into objects of seven inches diameter at the distance of two hundred and fifty yards … their shot have frequently proved fatal to British officers and soldiers, who expose themselves to view, even at more than double the distance of common musket shot. (Thatcher 1823: 38)

Congressman Richard Henry Lee praised "the dexterity to which they have arrived in the use of the Rifle Gun. Their [*sic*] is not one of those Men who wish a distance less than 200 yards or a larger object than an Orange – Every shot is fatal" (Lee 1859: 390). Another source claimed that the rifle company he witnessed "were entirely unacquainted with, and had never felt the passion of fear. With their rifles in their hands, they assume a kind of omnipotence over their enemies … there was not one who could not plug nineteen bullets out of twenty, as they termed it, within an inch of the head of a tenpenny nail" (Moore 1876: 122). Perhaps the most detailed account of the sharpshooting skills of the rifle companies comes from an anonymous letter written on August 1, 1775, and published in the *Pennsylvania Gazette*:

A clapboard, with a mark the size of a dollar, was put up; they began to fire off-hand, and the bystanders were surprised, few shots being made that were not close to or in the paper. When they had shot for a time in this way, some lay on their backs, some on their breast or side, others ran twenty or thirty steps, and firing, appeared to be equally certain of the mark. With this performance the company were more than satisfied, when a young man took up the board in his hand, not by the end, but by the side, and holding it up, his brother walked to the distance, and very coolly shot into the white; laying down his rifle, he took the board, and holding it as it was held before, the second brother shot as the former had done. By this exercise I was more astonished than pleased. But will you believe me, when I tell you, that one of the men took the board, and placing it between his legs, stood with his back to the tree while another drove the center. (Force 1840: 1)

A painting showing the death of Brigadier-General Simon Fraser at the battle of Bemis Heights on October 7, 1777. According to legend Fraser was shot and killed, by Patriot rifleman Timothy Murphy specifically on the orders of Major General Benedict Arnold, but there is no primary evidence to support this claim. (Hulton Archive/Getty Images)

This accuracy, while exaggerated in the newspapers of the time, did translate onto the battlefield. On occasion Patriot accuracy proved fatal for senior British officers. Brigadier-General James Webster was fatally wounded at the battle of Guilford Courthouse on March 15, 1781. More celebrated, from the American perspective, was the death of Brigadier-General Simon Fraser at the battle of Bemis Heights on October 7, 1777. The fatal shot has popularly been attributed to a single rifleman, Timothy Murphy, though there is no primary evidence of the shooter's identity. Nevertheless, Fraser was indeed shot and killed, and one American source recorded how "a number of our soldiers placed themselves in the boughs of high trees, in the rear and flanks, and took every opportunity of destroying the British officers by single shot" (Thatcher 1823: 118).

COMBAT | Private, Virginia rifle company

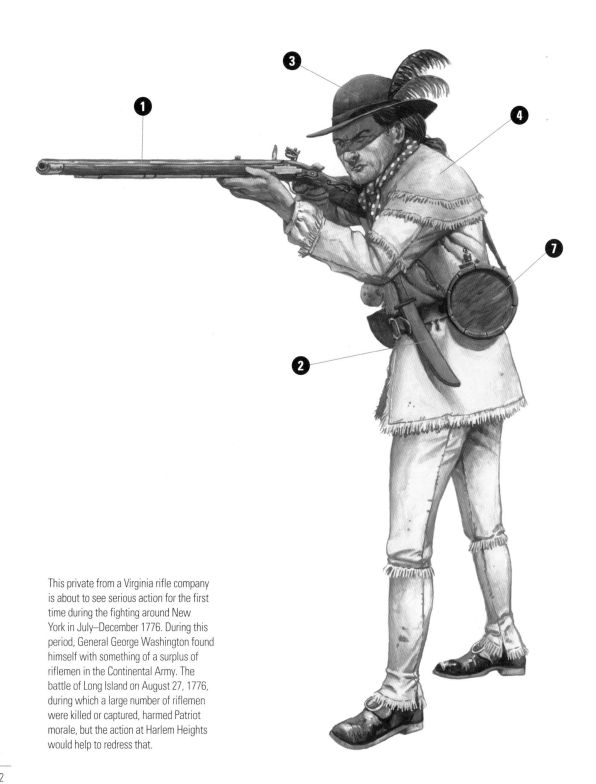

This private from a Virginia rifle company is about to see serious action for the first time during the fighting around New York in July–December 1776. During this period, General George Washington found himself with something of a surplus of riflemen in the Continental Army. The battle of Long Island on August 27, 1776, during which a large number of riflemen were killed or captured, harmed Patriot morale, but the action at Harlem Heights would help to redress that.

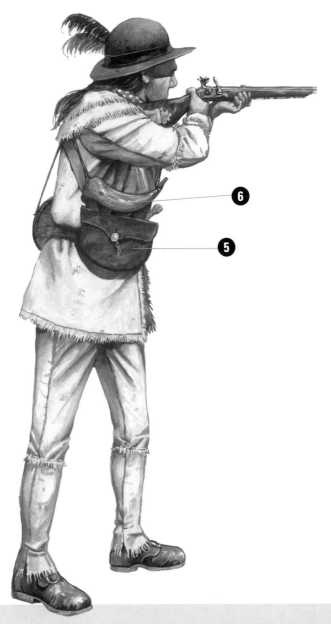

Weapons, dress, and equipment

This rifleman is armed with a "long" rifle (**1**), manufactured in Pennsylvania. These weapons were usually personally made and owned, though they were sometimes issued as military stores. Barrel length and caliber varied, with the latter ranging from .40 to .48. His only defense in close combat is his hunting knife (**2**), but some riflemen also carried hatchets.

He is outfitted in a style similar to the original rifle companies raised by Congress in 1775. His broad-brimmed hat (**3**) is decorated with feathers, though bear pelt was also sometimes used. His hunting shirt (**4**) is a light, loose garment that was closely associated with the frontier and the Patriot cause in general. While Patriot riflemen occasionally wore more formal military coats, the hunting shirt was the most common garment and was sometimes used by non-rifle regiments as well.

His ammunition is contained in a shot pouch (**5**) and a carved-bone powder horn (**6**). His canteen (**7**) is round and made of wood, though the Continental Army also made use of tin canteens. His knapsack, storing his personal belongings, has been discarded to aid his battlefield mobility.

Although there were instances of senior British officers being hit, it should be noted that the highest number of casualties suffered by the British officer corps in a single battle was at the battle of Bunker Hill on June 17, 1775, an engagement which saw the use of few to no rifled weapons by the Patriots – casualties were attributed by at least one source to the use of buckshot (Moore 1876: 121). In the eight years of fighting after Bunker Hill the British Army did not suffer notably higher casualties among its officers when compared with other 18th-century conflicts, a fact that implies the idea that American riflemen deliberately sniped officers with near-omnipotent accuracy was somewhat exaggerated. Indeed, at times Patriot commanders had to curb the enthusiasm of their riflemen. In 1776 Major General Charles Henry Lee complained to the commander of his rangers about how they had "been suffered to fire at a most preposterous distance," going on to demand that "not a man under your command is to fire at a greatest distance than an hundred and fifty yards, at the utmost; in short, that they never fire without almost a moral certainty of hitting their object" (Lee 1853: 501).

In order to achieve these levels of accuracy, it was necessary to wrap each rifle bullet in a small patch, usually made from leather, that allowed the bullet to grip the barrel as the rifle was fired, meaning it achieved the spin necessary for greater accuracy. This added extra complexities to the loading process, however, and therefore ensured that rifles were slower to fire than their smoothbore counterparts – one or two aimed shots a minute was most common.

Throughout the American Revolutionary War Patriot forces tended to possess firepower deemed superior to that of their enemies. This can be attributed at least in part to the use of rifles, most effectively employed in combination with troops armed with smoothbore muskets (Spring 2008: 204). This was evident in battles such as Guilford Courthouse, where a mixture of rifle- and smoothbore-armed Patriot militia delivered a devastating volley as the British advanced on the rail fence the Patriots were holding. Sergeant Roger Lamb of the 23rd Regiment of Foot recalled that "within forty yards of the enemy's line, it was perceived that their whole force had their arms presented, and resting on a rail fence ...They were taking aim with the

THIS PAGE & OPPOSITE
Three views of a Patriot rifle made *c.*1770 by an unknown manufacturer, possibly George Schreyer, Sr. of Hanover, Pennsylvania. As private arms, American rifles defied standardized specifications, but they tended to range in caliber from .40 to .48. (metmuseum.org/CC0 1.0)

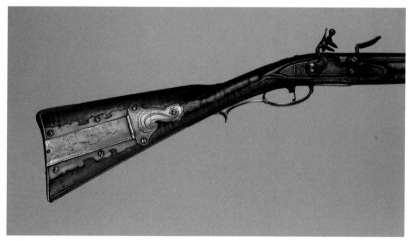

nicest precision" (Lamb 1809: 361). The ensuing fusillade inflicted perhaps as much as 50 percent casualties on one regiment.

The flintlock weaponry used by both sides was generally reliable, but became less effective in poor weather, especially rain. Rifles in particular did not fare well on campaign, being prone to breakages and requiring more cleaning maintenance. In combat, barrel fouling became a problem, with gunpowder residue making it particularly difficult to ram home ball-and-patch ammunition. This further reduced the riflemen's firepower and thus made them ineffective during prolonged engagements, such as the Hessian assault on the north face of Fort Washington in New York on November 16, 1776.

To compound these problems further, there was little in the way of standardization when it came to Patriot rifles. Many were individuals' personal property, and there was a lack of unity in terms of calibers. This made issues of storage and supply even more pronounced. Ammunition, for example, could not be supplied en masse as a single caliber, but would have to vary depending on the rifles with which individuals were equipped.

British

By contrast, light infantry armed with smoothbore muskets and premade cartridge ammunition could typically fire two or three aimed shots a minute. They could do so in open order, or in close-order formations when massed volleys were required. Nor were smoothbore muskets wholly outclassed at range – despite common misconceptions, light infantry could still engage effectively at up to 200yd, likely aided by the fact that experience and good marksmanship were among the preferred prerequisites for joining the light companies. Despite common misconceptions about the inaccuracy of smoothbore muskets and a reliance on massed volleys, standard British training inculcated the importance of well-placed shots. One book written to advise junior officers noted that recruits should "be taught to load and fire singly, that each man may be distinctly instructed in the proper methods of using a Cartridge … they should be taught to fire at marks, at different distances" (Cuthbertson 1776: 163–64). During peacetime live ammunition was carefully regulated and rarely available for regular practice, but that changed substantially during wartime. Civilians witnessed British troops practicing their accuracy in Boston in 1775, and likewise a British officer, Lieutenant Frederick Mackenzie of the 23rd Regiment of Foot (Royal Welsh Fuziliers), wrote on January 15, 1775, that soldiers practiced by shooting at targets (Mackenzie 1930: 28–29). One regiment, garrisoning a wharf by the harbor, placed floating life-sized targets out on the water, which provided challenging targets, and rewards were sometimes given for the best shots. This training resulted in some of the soldiers becoming very accurate with their firearms.

While the British Army in general did not neglect accuracy, light infantry in particular were expected to be among the best shots. Orders issued in 1772 instructed that "The Light Infantry are to be taught to fire at Marks, and each Soldier is to find out the proper Measure of Powder for his own Firelock and to make up his Cartridges accordingly" (Townshend

This light infantryman of the
33rd Regiment of Foot has been seconded
to the 3rd Light Battalion during the
New York campaign. Like all British
infantry, he fights with his bayonet fixed
– the weapon acquired as infamous a
reputation among Patriot soldiers as the
rifle did among the British.

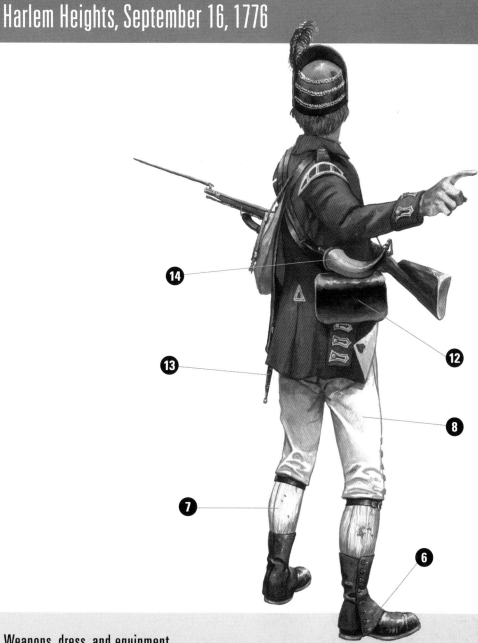

Weapons, dress, and equipment

The light infantryman is armed with a .75-caliber 1769 Short Land Pattern smoothbore flintlock musket (**1**). Standard issue to British light infantry, it featured a barrel 4in shorter than that of its predecessor, the Long Land Pattern. Fixed to the barrel is a 17in bayonet (**2**). British light infantry also carried hatchets, but there is scant evidence of their use in combat rather than as tools.

He wears his iconic leather cap (**3**) over hair cropped specifically for the campaign. Deemed more practical than the cocked hats of the line infantry, these caps were sometimes replaced by felt ones or cut-down hats. His jacket is shorter than the regimental coats of the line infantry, and has lace "wings" (**4**) that indicate that a soldier is either a grenadier or a light infantryman, part of the infantry's elite. Beneath the jacket is a sleeveless waistcoat (**5**). In some campaigns the light infantry did away with the jacket completely, sewing the jacket sleeves onto the waistcoat and wearing it instead of the jacket. The standard-issue half-gaiters (**6**), stockings (**7**), and breeches (**8**) were increasingly replaced by gaiter-trousers as the American Revolutionary War went on.

Over his right shoulder is a tin-plated canteen (**9**), secured by a length of cord. His haversack (**10**) carries up to three days' worth of rations. A pair of cross belts (**11**) in black leather, a light-infantry distinction, secure the cartridge pouch (**12**) and bayonet scabbard (**13**) respectively. The cartridge pouch has a leather flap protecting a wooden box holding prefabricated paper cartridges. Also attached to one of the belts is a cord holding a powder horn (**14**), but these generally do not seem to have been worn after the 1776 campaigns.

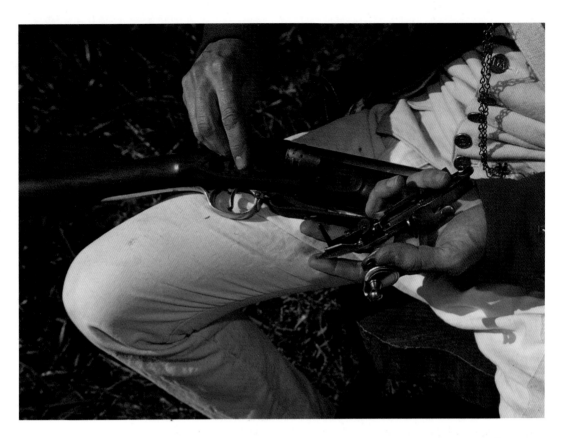

A re-enactor maintains a replica British smoothbore musket. Discharging a musket created a lot of gunpowder residue, which quickly led to rusting. Soldiers were therefore required to remove the musket's lock, and sometimes the entire barrel, from the stock as part of the cleaning process. This was generally a simpler process than keeping a rifle in working condition, with rifle barrels being more prone to fouling. Patriot commanders complained about the rifle's unsuitability to hard campaigning. (Fotosearch/Getty Images)

1894: 551). It was emphasized that the successful outcome of some combats may even come down to one well-placed round: "the Light Infantry Man, in particular, must not neglect his Arms, his Ammunition or throw away his Fire, as his Existence may depend upon a Single Shot's taking place" (Townshend 1894: 551).

As a further aid to accuracy, by 1777 some light infantrymen were armed not with smoothbore muskets, but with British- and Hanoverian-made rifles. These were manufactured in 1776, based not on the long American style but on the shorter German hunting rifles that became popular weapons among light infantry during the Seven Years' War. Produced in answer to the British government's concerns about Patriot riflemen, 1,000 of these rifles were subsequently distributed to British Army light companies and light dragoons. Loyalists of the Provincial Corps were also sometimes armed with rifles, with the Queen's Rangers counting an entire rifle company within their ranks.

While British light infantry did not experience the logistical issues associated with rifled weaponry, supply in general was a continual problem for Crown Forces throughout the war, exacerbated by a lack of support in the colonies and the sheer length of the Atlantic crossing. Cartridges of musket balls and gunpowder were made up by the regiment or by individual soldiers. Typically, the light infantryman carried between 36 and 60 rounds of ammunition into battle – enough for most regular troops – but the hard fighting experienced by light companies meant sufficient ammunition was sometimes lacking.

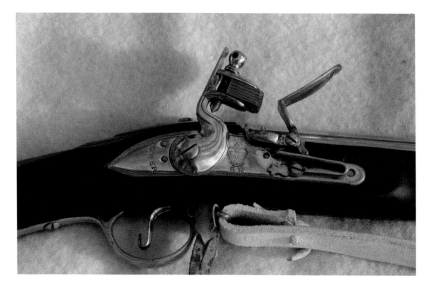

A replica musket lock showing the "Tower" inscription and the royal cipher. The flint has been replaced with a wooden square usually called a "driver" – these were used during drilling, so that repetitive dry-firing did not result in the flints needed for combat being worn down, or cause damage to the musket's hammer, which the flint struck to produce sparks. (Author's Collection)

CLOSE COMBAT

Patriot

The greatest weakness of American-manufactured rifles was their inability to mount a bayonet. While most European military rifles were made to be able to incorporate one, the long rifle's fragility meant it could not be used as a club. Furthermore, its lack of a bayonet left Patriot riflemen faced with combat at close quarters reliant on any hunting knives or hatchets they might carry.

This stark problem was further exacerbated by the rifle's other shortcoming – it took longer than a smoothbore musket to reload. The fact that the lead ball ammunition had to be wrapped in a leather pouch combined with a lack of prefabricated cartridges to mean even a skilled rifleman would struggle to manage two shots per minute. This in turn meant that riflemen alone were unable to lay down enough firepower to stop themselves being rushed by bayonet-armed troops – a tactic of which British light infantry were especially fond. One Hessian officer wrote mockingly that riflemen should be pitied rather than feared, as their weapon took so long to reload, they swiftly found themselves impaled by bayonets against the tree trunks they used as cover (Lowell 1884: 65–66).

The only feasible reaction to being charged was for riflemen to beat a precipitous retreat. At times, such as at the battle of Freeman's Farm on September 19, 1777, this tactic could actually prove highly effective. Charging soldiers inevitably spent themselves and came to a halt, at which point, if they had maintained a modicum of cohesion, the riflemen could cease retreating, turn, and resume attriting the enemy at range. There was little Crown Forces could do to counter this, and riflemen's persistence saw them likened to clouds of hornets by some British officers. This, however, relied on the riflemen being disciplined and courageous. Often when put to flight, however, riflemen simply didn't come back, especially if said riflemen were militiamen, whose general lack of training and combat experience often hampered Patriot efforts.

Depicted in 1812 in this portrait by Gilbert Charles Stuart (1755–1828), Henry Dearborn was born in New Hampshire in 1751. He joined the Continental Army at the outset of hostilities and served at the battle of Bunker Hill on June 17, 1775, and during the Quebec expedition of September–December 1775. He was given command of a force of Continental light infantry, and brigaded with Morgan's rifle corps for the Saratoga campaign of June–October 1777. While the use of bayonet-armed light infantry would have greatly assisted Morgan's riflemen at the battle of Freeman's Farm on September 19, 1777 (see pages 42–57), lack of time to train together beforehand would lead to mixed results and a lack of unit coordination. (Fotosearch/Getty Images)

Continental Army officers lamented the riflemen's lack of bayonets. An account concerning perhaps the most famous leader of riflemen during the war, Brigadier General Daniel Morgan, records him as claiming "my Riflemen would have been of little service if we had not always had a line of Musquet and Bayonette men to support us, it is this that gives them confidence. They know if the enemy charges them they have a place to retreat to and are not beat clear off" (quoted in Graham 1904: 135).

Major General Anthony Wayne put it even more firmly in a letter he wrote on February 8, 1778, to Richard Peters, Secretary of the Board of War, requesting that rifles in the Continental Army regiments he commanded be swapped for muskets and bayonets:

> I don't like rifles – I would almost as soon face an Enemy with a good Musket and Bayonet without amunition [*sic*] – as with amunition without a Bayonet for altho' there are not many Instances of bloody bayonets yet I am Confident that one bayonet keeps off an Other … the Enemy knowing the Defenseless State of our Riflemen rush on – they fly mix with or pass thro' the Other Troops and Communicate fears that is ever Incident to a retiring Corps – this Would not be the Case if the Riflemen had bayonets – but it would be still better if good muskets and bayonets were put into the hands of good Marksmen and Rifles entirely laid aslde – for my own part I never Wish to see one … I am so fully Convinced of the bad policy of such arms that no reasoning will ever Eradicate that Conviction. (Wayne 1893: 118)

Wayne was not the only one to request a change of armaments. On a number of occasions during the war, George Washington instructed rifle-armed troops to replace their weapons with smoothbore muskets and bayonets. Peters wrote on October 26, 1776, that rifles should be replaced by muskets "as they are more easily kept in order, can be fired oftener and have the advantage of Bayonetts" (quoted in Peters 1893: 405).

British

Unlike Patriot riflemen, British light infantry were equipped with bayonets and, like most British infantry during the American Revolutionary War, were encouraged to use them at every opportunity. The .75-caliber 1769 Short Land Pattern smoothbore flintlock muskets used by the light infantry took bayonets with blades that were generally 15–17in in length – fearsome-looking weapons that soon inspired as much dread in the Patriots as the rifle did in the British. By 1776 standard combat doctrine saw the British typically advance at speed, deliver one or two volleys, and then charge. This, they realized, was far preferable to becoming locked in a firefight, especially against riflemen. During the New York campaign of July–November 1776 General William Howe recommended "to the troops an entire dependence on their Bayonets with which they will always command that success which their bravery so well deserves" (Howe 1897: 35).

Light infantry in particular often looked to the bayonet, especially during raids and special operations. One military manual noted that "the light infantry of this army are to have their bayonets fixed, as the want of ammunition may sometimes be supplied by that weapon … it must be remembered, that bayonets are preferable to fire" (Simes 1768: 81). During the surprise attack by British forces at the battle of Paoli on September 20, 1777, the light infantry went into battle with bayonets fixed and muskets unloaded, possibly with the flints removed. This was mainly to ensure an accidental discharge didn't give the attack away, but it also forced the British to rely on the use of bayonets alone, ensuring the attack was driven home with maximum aggression. This was indeed what happened, with Major John André describing how the light infantry "rushed along the line putting to the bayonet all they came up with, and, overtaking the main herd of the fugitives, stabbed great numbers and pressed on their rear till it was thought prudent to order them to desist" (André 1903: 94). A similar outcome occurred on September 27, 1778, at Old Tappan, New Jersey, where light infantry surprised Continental Army dragoons in their billets and put the majority of them to the bayonet.

Besides bayonets, British light infantry were nominally issued with hatchets. These seem to have been tools rather than weapons, however, and there is limited evidence that they were carried into battle. Evidence of the use of modified bayonets with the .62-caliber Pattern 1776 rifle is also lacking, though the German *Jäger* were often armed with short swords known as *Hirschfänger* ('deer catchers'). A single company of *Jäger* from Hessen-Hanau were also documented as being armed with sword-bayonets that could be fitted to their rifles.

DISCIPLINE

Patriot

The newly raised rifle companies were to be the first units of the Continental Army, and their officers were appointed via the approval of the Continental Congress in a style that would have been familiar in Europe. Despite this, the rifle companies did not initially conform to the standards of regular soldiers, and both officers and men were unfamiliar with standard military discipline. Indeed, not long after joining the large militia force that besieged Boston from April 1775 through March 1776, the newly raised rifle companies became known for a degree of indiscipline. This was attributed largely to the fact that their ranks were composed of frontiersmen and volunteers unfamiliar with the rigors of an 18th-century military force. Due to their reputation as elite troops, the rifle companies were excused the more mundane duties such as latrine maintenance or acting as sentries, but with little enemy contact they quickly grew restless, and the rest of the Continental Army began to question their usefulness. Discipline started to deteriorate.

Matters came to a head when a sergeant in one of the rifle companies was incarcerated for insubordination. His compatriots responded by breaking into the jail and releasing a prisoner held there. This man was recaptured and taken to a more secure location. Fearing an outright mutiny, Washington ordered 500 Continentals to protect the jail. The

A present-day replica bayonet. Those employed by troops armed with smoothbore muskets on both sides tended to have blades at least 15in long, and which did not impede the loading of a firearm. Their fearsome appearance rendered them even more effective as psychological as well as practical weapons. (Author's Collection)

ruckus eventually abated, but the damage to the riflemen's standing in the army around Boston had been done. One Continental Army officer, Colonel John Thomas, delivered a damning verdict, stating that the riflemen were "as Indifferent men as I ever served with. These privates are mutinous, and often deserting to the enemy; unwilling for duty of any kind; exceedingly vicious; and, I think, the army here would be as well without as with them" (Thomas 1883: 338). Desertion seems to have been a problem, and there were even accounts of riflemen joining the British and taking their weapons with them – one soldier was sent with his rifle to London to be viewed by King George III.

Following the initial shock of entering military life, the rifle companies settled into a more disciplined pattern of service. Washington noted in 1776 that his riflemen were "a valuable and brave body of men" and that they "are indeed a very useful corps" (Washington 1796: 122). Units such as the rifle corps raised by Daniel Morgan were as well-disciplined as other regiments, likely because they were composed of picked men who had already served elsewhere in the Continental Army. A general order issued by Washington on June 1, 1777, specified that rifle units were not only "to include none but such as are known to be perfectly skilled in the use of these guns" but that the men should also be "known to be active and orderly in their behaviour" (Washington 1933: 156). Similarly, the rifle-armed companies that formed part of some Continental Army regiments were subject to the same regular discipline, and did not receive preferential treatment. This went a long way to rehabilitating the image of riflemen throughout the Continental Army.

British

The discipline of 18th-century military life was in itself not an issue for British light infantry. Composed as they were of experienced regular soldiers, the light-infantry companies tended to adhere to the norms of the Army's codes of conduct. One modern author has postulated that some light-infantry units experienced fewer incidents of desertion than regular line infantry did (Spring 2008: 59). There were occasions, however, when discipline also proved challenging for the light infantry, though the reasons were often different from those of the Patriots. The level of antipathy felt toward the Patriots by light infantrymen caused a high level of aggression during combat, and sometimes atrocities were committed when attacking Patriot positions. At the battle of Paoli officers had to order their men to desist from bayoneting the enemy, while at Old Tappan Patriot accounts claimed that British junior officers actually encouraged the murder of Patriot prisoners, in defiance of the repeated orders of more senior command figures to show restraint when dealing with enemy prisoners. While such brutality underscored the light infantry's reputation, it also badly undermined wider British efforts to bring the American Revolutionary War to a peaceful conclusion. Similarly, when peace was rumored in 1779 the light infantry exhibited a near-mutinous streak.

Light infantry were also guilty of rapaciousness when it came to foraging. Looting and the destruction of American property was a continual issue,

and one in which the light infantry appear to have taken pride. In the same way that company-level officers appear to have actively encouraged their men's bloodlust in defiance of standing orders, so too did certain officers champion their men's looting even as senior commanders attempted to win the hearts and subdue the minds of the rebelling colonists. One officer of the 52nd Regiment of Foot's light company, Lieutenant Martin Hunter, boasted that his men were "famous providers. They were good hands at a grab … I am very certain there never was a more expert set than the light infantry at either grab, lob ["grab" and "lob" were terms used to describe plundering], or gutting a house" (Hunter 1894: 27). Exasperated orders from above relating to looting were not uncommon – in 1778, for example, Lieutenant-Colonel Robert Abercromby, commanding officer of the 37th Regiment of Foot, warned that those of his men caught plundering would be severely punished, and demanded that officers give up any offenders rather than shield them (Coote 2011). Similarly, during the fighting in the South Major Patrick Ferguson complained about the fact that, because the light infantry were typically the advance guard of the army, they were always the first to come upon fresh food and supplies, and often gorged themselves on it (Urwin 2019: 11).

In all of these aspects the light infantry displayed characteristics that are frequently associated with elite fighting formations. Soldiers possessed a strong *esprit de corps* and a firm belief in their superiority over friend and foe alike. Due to the shared experience of frequent front-line combat, officers and men bonded more closely than in other outfits and in cases where light infantrymen flouted the British Army's wider rules, it seems that company-level officers were sometimes prepared to overlook their excesses.

ABOVE LEFT
A view of personal gear carried by a re-enactor. Like all British Army foot soldiers, the light infantryman carried a haversack with food (usually three days' worth) and a water canteen, often made from tin, into combat. The knapsack was almost always left behind before entering action, though soldiers would frequently carry their blanket rolls with them. (Author's Collection)

ABOVE RIGHT
Lieutenant-General William Howe, depicted in this contemporary illustration, served as a British light-infantry commander during the Seven Years' War and, as commander-in-chief of British land forces in North America during the American Revolutionary War, spread his light-infantry doctrines to the entire army operating there. (Fotosearch/Getty Images)

CONDUCT IN BATTLE

Patriot

The battle of Long Island on August 27, 1776, is depicted in this painting. The battle saw British forces surprise and rout a large section of the Continental Army. A wide flanking maneuver spearheaded by British light infantry resulted in numerous Patriot riflemen being killed or captured. The main body of the Continental Army narrowly escaped entrapment on the Brooklyn Heights, and subsequently lost New York city, failing to regain the initiative as they were forced to abandon first Manhattan Island, and then the area north of New York city as well, withdrawing all the way through New Jersey on the far side of the Hudson River. (Hulton Archive/Getty Images)

Much like their British light-infantry opponents, Patriot riflemen were taught to employ skirmishing tactics. The tactics' emphasis drew part, though not all, of their legacy from operations both against and alongside Native Americans during earlier conflicts, such as the Seven Years' War. Partisan and militia groups in particular used this "Indian" style of fighting, preferring to engage in forests. When an enemy force was located and pinned, riflemen would seek out their flanks and use a "half-moon" formation to attempt a partial envelopment. Such a style of fighting required discipline and coordination, not least because it was difficult for one "prong" of the formation to communicate with the other. Often an enemy bayonet charge could collapse the formation, but the most effective rifle units knew when to give ground and could then return to the action later. The battle of Kings Mountain on October 7, 1780, offers perhaps the best example of such tactics, with rifle-armed Patriot militia steadily surrounding and ultimately annihilating a strong Loyalist force in wooded terrain.

Rifleman also operated in pairs or small groups not only in battle, but during guerrilla activity. These teams would leave their encampments often at night and snipe at British sentries and pickets, retreating before reprisals could be organized. This tactic was most frequently employed in fighting in

24

A portrait of General George Washington. Like many senior officers and politicians, Washington initially had high hopes for the rifle companies raised in 1775. While those hopes were dashed by indiscipline, over the course of the American Revolutionary War Washington was aware of the importance of balancing the number of riflemen available to the Continental Army – fielding too many jeopardized the effectiveness of linear combat, but too few removed a valuable tactical edge. (metmuseum.org/CC0 1.0)

New Jersey in the early months of 1777, but was practiced to some degree throughout the American Revolutionary War.

While the practice was not universal, some units of Patriot riflemen used horns for signals, relying on them to carry more clearly than drumbeats in broken terrain and to reach troops dispersed during skirmishing. More unusual instruments were also used. During one expedition Patriots made use of conch shells to convey signals, and during a lull in the fighting at Freeman's Farm Patriot commander Colonel Daniel Morgan rallied his scattered riflemen with a device that imitated the call of a turkey. Commanders therefore came up with inventive methods of attempting to extend their ability to control their forces over a wide area.

British

Light infantry were trained to employ skirmish tactics, making intelligent use of cover, be it houses, walls and fences, boulders, or trees. Formed in two ranks, soldiers typically operated alongside their file partners in pairs, one loading while the other fired. This could be done while advancing or withdrawing. "To tree" entered the British Army's vocabulary as an instruction partially to break formation and take advantage of the cover offered in woodland and forests. This became familiar practice for light infantrymen during the first two years of the American Revolutionary War.

When a light battalion entered battle it was not expected always to operate as a single, cohesive unit. This was certainly possible, and was common practice – light infantry were able to operate in close order as line infantry, in two or even four ranks. With the difficult terrain in North America necessitating that even line infantry usually fought in open order, however, light infantry took full advantage of the freedom given to company commanders. Depending on the nature of the battlefield, light companies could break from their battalion "parent," attacking or retreating depending on local conditions and moving to aid other units when necessary. This flexibility was in evidence in the fighting at Birmingham Hill during the battle of Brandywine on September 11, 1777, where individual light companies used their initiative to outflank and drive back multiple Patriot units, using terrain such as walls, gullies, and forests to their advantage.

The downside of this dispersed method of fighting was that command and control became problematic. It proved difficult to maintain the cohesion of even a company of troops while dispersed in woodland. The situation was not helped by the fact that the British Army tended to have a low ratio of officer and NCOs to enlisted men when compared with the Continental Army. Controlling tactical engagements was therefore no simple matter for small-unit leaders.

As with the Patriot riflemen, British light-infantry companies used several methods to solve this problem. Most obvious was the fact that the musicians in a light company used horns or bugles, rather than drums, for sending signals. The instruments' sound carried more effectively than that of drums, and could be used to convey orders that would be heard by soldiers dispersed during a forest fight. Some light-infantry officers also made use of whistles. This was not standard practice, but whistles were employed by some enterprising officers who taught their men to react to different whistle signals. It was noted that Captain Matthew Johnson of the 46th Regiment of Foot's light company, employed a whistle to signal to his men, using it not only to give directions about formations, but also to indicate when they should take cover and return fire. This was reportedly done to great effect during the fighting at Harlem Heights, when the company crouched while the Patriots delivered a volley, then at the direction of Johnson's whistle rose to return fire (Spring 2008: 190). Similarly, Lieutenant-Colonel Patrick Ferguson employed a whistle alongside specific gestures made by waving his hat. In this way it seems some British officers were still able to issue commands and exert authority over an extended or broken battle space.

REPUTATION

Patriot

From the start of the American Revolutionary War, Patriot riflemen possessed a fearsome reputation among friend and foe alike. In 1775 in particular, onlookers were often awed by the appearance and apparent hardiness of the rifle companies. One described them as "remarkably stout and hardy men; many of them exceeding six feet in height" (Thatcher 1823: 37–38). Congressman Lee praised "their amazing hardihood, their method of living so long in the woods without carrying provisions with them, the exceeding quickness with which they can march to distant parts" (Lee 1859: 390). Another gentleman described "a formidable company of upwards of one hundred and thirty men, from the mountains and back-woods, painted like Indians, armed with tomahawks and rifles, dressed in hunting-shirts and moccasins … Health and vigour, after what they had undergone, declared them to be intimate with hardship and familiar with danger" (Force 1840: 1). John Adams, one of the Founding Fathers and a member of the Committee of Five that drafted the Declaration of Independence, claimed that the riflemen were "Men of Property and Family, some of them of independent Fortunes, who go from the purest Motives of Patriotism and Benevolence into this service" (Adams 1917: 76). During this period, Patriot riflemen were considered to be potential paragons of liberty and warriors with few peers. This view was, of course, at best somewhat misplaced, and problems with discipline as well as the limitations of the rifle as an actual weapon soon altered this perception in the eyes of military commanders and leading politicians.

A view of the recreated 10th Regiment of Foot's light infantry delivering a volley. Note some of the distinctive features of the British light infantry: the small, round black leather caps with chains; the white shoulder lace; and the black leather belting. Black-powder weapons quickly shrouded the battlefield in smoke, and this combined with the nature of terrain in North America – often hilly, or forested – to make traditional linear warfare even more difficult to practice. This was where light infantry came into their own, able to act loosely and on their own initiative or that of their company commanders. (Adrien Bisson/ Alamy Stock Photo)

While the discipline problems – drunkenness, brawling, desertion, and a lack of respect for authority – that resulted when the riflemen joined the rest of the Continental Army tempered the esteem in which they were held by their countrymen, the reputation of riflemen with the public remained fearsome. Patriot newspapers in particular not only praised the riflemen but directed dire warnings toward the British. *The Virginia Gazette* boasted of a rifleman killing his target at 400yd and mockingly advised British soldiers to take care (Scribner 1973: 9). Another piece published in *The London Chronicle* warned that 1,000 riflemen had been raised, and that British officers should settle their affairs before leaving for America, with the obvious inference that they wouldn't survive an encounter with rifle-armed Patriots (Evensen 2018: 58).

This reputation couldn't fail to have an effect on Crown Forces soldiers. One light-infantry officer, Captain William Dansey of the 33rd Regiment of Foot, wrote that at home "our good Friends thought we were all to be kill'd with Rifles" (Dansey 2010: 20). Soldiers and officers alike worried about Patriot marksmanship and the enemy's irregular style of partisan warfare. Pickets were sometimes enlarged and tactics were often altered, with traps being set, for example posting lone sentries in order to lure in riflemen. Crown Forces riflemen, whether in British light companies or Hessian *Jäger* companies, were employed to counter the threat posed. A German officer wrote that "the rebels lurk in the woods and dart from tree to tree … their riflemen are terrible," though his observation was tempered by the claim that "they respect, however, the prowess of our riflemen," and also the fact that, in this case, the terrible aspect being described was the use of buckshot to cause multiple wounds, rather than fearsome accuracy (Stone 1891: 90–91). After the battle of Long Island on August 27, 1776, when 200 Patriot riflemen were captured, their rifles were seized from them and broken apart on the spot by British soldiers (Spring 2008: 135). A Patriot source also claimed that "where they found a rifleman resisting too long, they pinned him with their bayonets, and to some of the wounded they showed no mercy" (Johnston 1878: 185). A Royal Navy officer was recorded as writing of the hatred exhibited toward riflemen, and how the slowness of their chosen weapon hampered them, for "before they are able to make a second discharge, it frequently happens that they find themselves run through the body by the push of a bayonet, as a rifleman is not entitled to any quarter" (Moore 1876: 350). British regulars certainly seem to have despised foes that they viewed as straying beyond the accepted norms of period warfare.

Continental Army officers were aware that their riflemen carried a deadly reputation among the enemy. Charles Lee wrote that "It is a certain truth, that the enemy entertain a most fortunate apprehension of American riflemen" (Lee 1853: 501), clearly aware of the fact that rifles had an impact on British morale. Washington, when confronted with clothing issues for his men in 1776, considered the possibility of garbing them in hunting shirts, partly because they were cheap and practical, but also due to the fact that such clothing was the typical attire of the riflemen, and was therefore "justly supposed to carry no small terror to the enemy, who thinks every such person a complete marksman" (Washington 1881: 147). The psychological impact of the rifle was clear.

THE AMERICAN RIFLE MEN.

At the beginning of hostilities in the American Revolutionary War, close-fitting black cloth half-gaiters – smart, but impractical in the difficult terrain of North America – were part of the uniform for British light infantry. Worn at the battle of Harlem Heights on September 16, 1776, they were frequently superseded by gaitered trousers after the first few years of the war. (Author's Collection)

British

While riflemen and their weapon of choice elicited fear and loathing among Crown Forces, Patriots experienced the same emotions when confronted by British light infantry. It was generally acknowledged that, along with grenadiers, the light-infantry companies that formed part of the regular battalions were the best troops in the British Army. Period literature spelled out that they were expected to be competent marksmen, physically capable, courageous, and independent in spirit. One set of instructions advised that, concerning the recruitment of light infantry, "it is therefore necessary to be particular in selecting Men for this Service not only of Activity and Bodyly Strength but also of some Experience and approved Spirit" (Townshend

A cartoon showing portly light infantrymen on the move. Cartoonists in Britain were also scathing of the supposed virtues of light infantry, often depicting such soldiers – these are volunteers raised from home defense rather than service in North America – as portly and unfit. These men are marching with muskets "at the trail," a staple of light-infantry drill and intended for movement amid broken terrain. (Anne S.K. Brown Military Collection, Brown University Library)

1894: 551). Another military author advised that the light infantry "were composed of both Officers and soldiers, whose health, strength and activity could be most depended upon" (Simes 1768: 316). A third held the view that light infantry were "to be composed of chosen men, whose activity and particular talents for that duty should be the only recommendation to their appointment" (Cuthbertson 1776: 190).

Once in action, the light infantry swiftly gained a reputation for speed and ruthlessness on the attack. Patriots applied the nickname "bloodhounds" to them, based on the way in which they aggressively hunted down their enemies, including Patriot riflemen. The light infantry were celebrated in song, with one verse written in 1778 highlighting how, "as fierce as the tiger, as swift as the roe, the British Light Infantry rush on their foe," and that "though rebels unnumber'd oppose their career, their hearts are undaunted; they're strangers to fear" (Moore 1856: 204–05). Young officers who sought advancement through action applied to join the light companies, knowing that they would always be at the heart of the action, while the light companies themselves often had the pick of the best soldiers from among their parent battalions.

The prospect of fighting light infantry had a detrimental impact on Patriot morale. During one surprise attack, "one of the rebel officers, demanding the name of the corps which had attacked them, was answered 'The British light infantry,' on which he exclaimed, 'Then we shall all be cut off'" (Moore 1876: 622). Conversely, after a series of stinging defeats and alleged atrocities, Continental Army Lieutenant Colonel Adam Hubley of the 10th Pennsylvania Regiment wrote of how aggressively his men attacked light infantry at the battle of Germantown on October 4, 1777. According to Hubley, the Continentals' eagerness to gain revenge over their usually dominant foes caused them to attack with the bayonet and eschew taking prisoners (McGuire 2000: 174). Later accounts claimed that the light infantry took to sporting red hackles as a mark of pride following the Paoli attack, or to better help the Patriots locate the troops against whom they had sworn vengeance. Regardless of whether they inspired fear or fury, the reputation of the British light infantry preceded them as surely as that of the Patriot riflemen they sometimes found themselves engaging.

Harlem Heights

September 16, 1776

BACKGROUND TO BATTLE

On August 27, 1776, British forces defeated the Patriot forces on Long Island, forcing their withdrawal to Manhattan Island. On September 15, in an effort to cut Manhattan Island in half, British troops landed on its east bank, at Kip's Bay. Crown Forces completed the landing successfully, but advanced slowly, allowing Washington to evacuate his army from New York and withdraw to the heights at the northern end of the island.

The British spread out across the island facing the new Patriot positions. The light-infantry battalions were posted between the main regimental encampments and those of the enemy on Harlem Heights. British light infantry had played an important part in encountering and soundly defeating riflemen during the battle of Long Island. Morale was high, and the light battalions appeared convinced of their own abilities. Conversely, the mood in the Patriot camp, following successive withdrawals, was downbeat. Washington feared an immediate British attack on his new positions and, with only the crossing at King's Bridge offering a safe route of escape to the north, the danger of being cut off and destroyed – as had nearly happened at Long Island – seemed very real.

The two British light battalions that would be engaged on September 16 were the 2nd and 3rd, with the 1st posted farther south. All three were ad hoc composite units created by detaching the light companies from each of the regular battalions in General William Howe's army around New York. This practice had become common during the Seven Years' War, and Howe himself had commanded a light battalion during the British capture of Quebec on September 13, 1759. The 2nd Light Battalion was formed from the light companies detached from the 40th, 43rd, 44th, 45th, 52nd, 55th, 63rd, and

This painting shows British and German troops marching through the streets of New York. The day prior to the battle of Harlem Heights the British entered the city, just hours after it had been abandoned by Washington and the Continental Army. (MPI/Getty Images)

64th regiments of Foot, while the 3rd Light Battalion was composed of the companies belonging to the 15th, 28th, 33rd, 37th, 46th, 54th, and 57th regiments of Foot. Their strength by the time of Harlem Heights was about 300 effectives per battalion. While in 1776 Howe's army in general could not be considered experienced campaigners, the light companies included the ablest soldiers, and operations in 1775 as well as the battle of Long Island had given them a valuable understanding of fighting in America, including the confidence to engage their enemies in woodland skirmishing. As the action at Harlem Heights developed these light battalions were supported by Hessian *Jäger* riflemen, the British 42nd and 33rd regiments of Foot, and composite grenadier battalions, as well as two field guns manned by the Royal Artillery. These troops taken in total composed the British advanced corps, the army's elite.

Like the British light battalions, Knowlton's Rangers were a composite force composed of picked men drawn from a number of different Continental Army and State units, mostly the Connecticut regiments of Durkee, Webb, Chester, Parsons, and Wyllys, and from Sargent's and Nixon's Massachusetts regiments. Knowlton's Rangers were formed on August 12, 1776, with the intention of providing the Continental Army with troops able to perform scouting, reconnaissance, and other light-infantry roles. The officers were chosen personally by Lieutenant Colonel Thomas Knowlton, a veteran of both the Seven Years' War and the battle of Bunker Hill. They were almost certainly armed with smoothbore muskets, rather than rifles. Riflemen were not in short supply for the Continental Army during the New York campaign, however – there were around 2,000 present among Washington's forces. During the battle of Harlem Heights the rangers were supported for much of the engagement by three companies of the 3rd Virginia Regiment. Raised on December 28, 1775, this Continental Army outfit, like the other early Virginian regiments, included a mixture of rifle- and smoothbore-armed companies, with the former expected to operate as light infantry. As the fighting developed during the day more Continental Army regiments, likely including more riflemen, came up to support the rangers and Virginians, along with artillery.

MAP KEY

1 *c.*0700hrs: Lieutenant Colonel Thomas Knowlton's rangers encounter pickets belonging to the British 2nd Light Infantry Battalion near the Jones farmhouse. After a skirmish the rangers are driven back to the Patriot lines.

2 *c.*0930hrs: The light infantry halt above the Hollow Way as Washington deploys troops to draw them into a trap.

3 *c.*1100hrs: Knowlton's Rangers and two rifle companies from the 3rd Virginia Regiment commanded by Major Andrew Leitch are sent to outflank the light infantry and attack from the rear. After getting lost, the Patriots accidentally attack the British in the flank. After a sharp skirmish the light infantry fall back to a buckwheat field.

4 *c.*1200hrs: The British light infantry rally in the buckwheat field as reinforcements from the light battalions, the 42nd Regiment of Foot, and some artillery and Hessians come up. Also reinforced, the Patriots engage across the field in a prolonged firefight. Eventually the British retreat once more.

5 *c.*1400hrs: Elements of the 42nd Foot make a stand in an orchard, but cannot stop the oncoming Patriots. The Americans halt just past the orchard and, seeing further British reinforcements approaching, retire back to their own lines.

Battlefield environment

The armies' advance guards were separated by a little under 2 miles. The British pickets were stationed near a stone-built farmhouse belonging to one Nicholas Jones, sited on a low hill. Beyond it, about 700yd farther north, was an orchard, and past that the terrain became "the wooded and rolling grounds of the two farms on the Morningside Heights" (Johnston 1897: 58). These two farms, belonging to the Vandewater and Hoaglandt families respectively, lay close to the west bank of Manhattan Island, almost bordering the Hudson River. Near the middle of this area of small hills and forests was a circular field that, in September 1776, was full of buckwheat.

About a half-mile before reaching the Patriot lines the Morningside Heights dropped away into a valley, a depression known as the Hollow Way and including a path running almost parallel between the two armies to its terminus at a landing point on the western shore of Manhattan Island. On the north side of the Hollow Way, at the start of the Waldron estate, the ground rose and became forested once again, marking the start of the Patriot lines on Harlem Heights.

The terrain over which the ensuing battle was fought was therefore quite broken, and the forests and rises, interspersed with the fences separating the Vandewater and Hoaglandt estates, all combined to make traditional 18th-century combat, as well as regular command and control, challenging. Conversely, it was almost exactly the sort of battlefield on which both British light infantry and Patriot riflemen were expected to operate best.

This depiction of the area near New York city in 1776 gives a good indication of the sort of terrain fought over during the battle of Harlem Heights – undulating, with outcrops of trees and rocks interspersed with small fields and farmsteads, all next to the Hudson River. (Fotosearch/Getty Images)

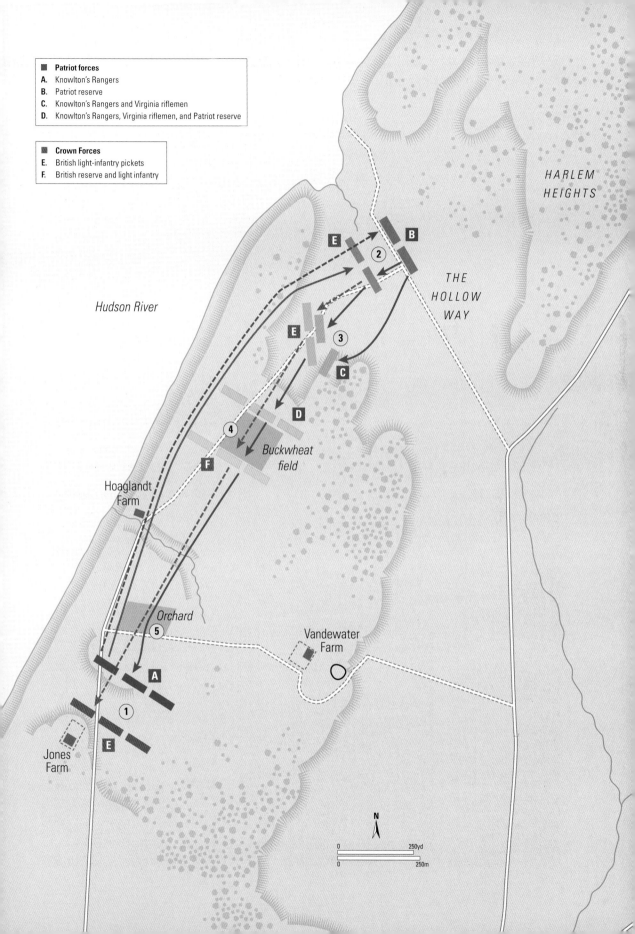

Patriot forces
A. Knowlton's Rangers
B. Patriot reserve
C. Knowlton's Rangers and Virginia riflemen
D. Knowlton's Rangers, Virginia riflemen, and Patriot reserve

Crown Forces
E. British light-infantry pickets
F. British reserve and light infantry

HARLEM
HEIGHTS

Hudson River

THE
HOLLOW
WAY

E

B

2

E

3

C

D

4

Buckwheat
field

F

Hoaglandt
Farm

Orchard

Vandewater
Farm

5

A

1

E

Jones
Farm

N

0   250yd
0   250m

INTO COMBAT

On September 16, the day after the British landing at Kip's Bay, Washington became concerned that Crown Forces were about to launch an assault on his newly established lines across Harlem Heights. He ordered forward Knowlton and his rangers, a force of 150 men, giving them instructions to reconnoiter the British positions and give advance warning of any possible attack. They set out at dawn, moving up onto the Morningside Heights.

In reality there was no British offensive planned for that day. At around 0700hrs, however, Knowlton's rangers ran into the British light infantry acting as advance pickets close to the Jones farmhouse. Two British companies responded to the initial Patriot fire, and a skirmish began. For over a half-hour "the woods along the dividing line between Jones' and Hoaglandt's farms rang with sharp firing from both sides" (Johnston 1897: 61–62). The brisk engagement lasted long enough to draw the attention of both armies.

Having felt out the rangers' strength and dispositions, the light infantry began to extend their skirmish line in order to outflank the Patriots. Realizing what was happening, Knowlton ordered his rangers to break off the engagement and retreat. They did so in good order, with the light infantry immediately mounting a rapid pursuit. The rangers evacuated the woodland and fell back through the Hollow Way. Beyond it they were able to regroup under the protection of the Continental main lines. The light infantry hounded them as far as the edge of the Hollow Way, where they too halted to regroup, satisfied that they had driven the enemy back to their own defenses. During the fighting one of Washington's subordinates, Colonel Joseph Reed, heard the sound of the light infantry's horns calling the companies to re-form. He mistook the notes for those used during a fox hunt, however, a fact that at once shamed him with its implication of cowardice and is commonly thought to have hardened the Continentals' resolve.

Realizing that the light infantry had overextended themselves and were now considerably closer to the Patriot lines than to their own, Washington formulated a plan to entrap and destroy the detachment. While reinforcements from the main line occupied the light infantry's attention, Knowlton's rangers, reinforced by three rifle companies from Colonel George Weedon's 3rd Virginia Regiment, planned to take a circuitous route across the Hollow Way and come up on the light infantry's rear, thereby entrapping and destroying them.

According to Captain Gustavus Brown Wallace, Weedon's Virginians had been "kept under arms the whole night, and in the morning about 9 o'clock we heard our picquet guard [Knowlton's] … attacked by

A stirring depiction of Captain Thomas Knowlton. Born in Massachusetts on November 22, 1740, Knowlton played a prominent role at the battle of Bunker Hill. On August 12, 1776, he was promoted to lieutenant colonel and given command of a composite force of light infantry, or rangers, by Washington. These picked troops, known as Knowlton's Rangers, engaged British light infantry at the start of the battle of Harlem Heights, and spent much of the day fighting alongside Virginian riflemen. Knowlton was killed during the action. This romanticized depiction of Knowlton at Bunker Hill shows him with a loose shirt and bared breast, facing the oncoming British head-on. (Sepia Times/ Universal Images Group via Getty Images)

A photograph taken on the site of Harlem Heights. While the battlefield is now almost entirely lost to Manhattan's sprawl, a number of photos were taken at the close of the 19th century, before the area became heavily urbanized. These images give a sense of what the Morningside Heights were like around the time of the battle. This image shows the Bloomingdale Road, which partially cut through the action, facing north toward the Continental Army lines. (Classic Collection 3/Alamy Stock Photo)

the enemy"; they were "drawn up in a small field that we had been in all night and about five or six minutes after we saw the picquet guard running like the d---l, on which we were ordered to advance" (quoted in Johnston 1897: 119).

Three rifle companies, led by captains Charles West, John Thornton, and John Ashby and placed under the command of Major Andrew Leitch, were singled out and attached to Knowlton's Rangers once they had re-formed. The combined force was, according to Wallace, ordered "to cross the swamp above the meadow and flank the enemy" (quoted in Johnston 1897: 119). This they began to do, working round the light infantry from the east. At the same time Washington ordered forward the diversionary force. He reported how the light infantry took the bait and "immediately ran down the hill, and took possession of some fences and bushes, and a smart firing began" (quoted in Johnston 1897: 130).

The British met the diversion in the Hollow Way in skirmish formation, anchoring their position along a fence line. The Patriots opened fire prematurely, but it seems the weight of their musketry may have been enough to drive the two British companies back – possibly too soon. Reed, who had been tasked with guiding the rangers and riflemen around the flank of the British, claimed that the riflemen took the wrong route and, unable to divert them, he found that they had fallen in with the flank of the light companies, rather than their rear: "some of our Troops in another Quarter moved up towards the Enemy & the Action began" (quoted in Johnston 1897: 137). Washington described how "the parties under Colonel Knowlton and Major Leitch unluckily began their attack too soon, as it was rather in the flank than in the rear" (quoted in Johnston 1897: 130).

The action, until that point carried out at long range between the light infantry and the forces involved in the diversionary attack, grew more intense.

Some of the rocky elevation visible in this late-19th-century photo of the battlefield of Harlem Heights indicates where the rifle flank attack on the British light infantry occurred. At the time the elevation was more forested. (Classic Collection 3/Alamy Stock Photo)

William Dansey

William Dansey was born William Collins in Herefordshire, England, in about 1745. His father, Dansey Collins, was a member of the local gentry and a captain in the 33rd Regiment of Foot. During the Seven Years' War William Dansey joined his father's regiment, initially as a volunteer, acquiring a commission as an ensign on July 30, 1760. He was involved in campaigns in the German states before being deployed to the Mediterranean garrison island of Minorca in 1764. In 1766 he was appointed a lieutenant in the 33rd Foot, making him the youngest officer to hold that rank in the regiment. The 33rd Foot returned to Britain in 1770 – a relief to Dansey, who found garrison life dull.

In January 1776 Dansey was given command of the 33rd Foot's light company, a prestigious appointment. His first action during the American Revolutionary War occurred when his transport ship encountered a Patriot vessel off the coast of North Carolina, resulting in a successful capture. He led the regiment's light company during the New York campaign, where he had a number of close encounters with Patriot riflemen. He was

ultimately dismissive of his opponents, finding them to be not as fearsome shots as many officers had been led to believe. He was involved in the fighting at Harlem Heights, where he was part of the 3rd Light Battalion, which came to the aid of the embattled 2nd Light Battalion in the buckwheat field. He described being in the heat of the action, a prolonged and intensive firefight that he considered himself fortunate to escape unhurt. His light company suffered one man killed and three injured, including a sergeant and a lieutenant.

Dansey commanded the 33rd Foot's light company until 1778, when he was promoted to the rank of major. He missed the Crown Forces' surrender at Yorktown on October 19, 1781, and was tasked with reassembling the remnants of the 33rd Foot as an effective fighting force, a duty in which he appears largely to have succeeded. He was promoted to lieutenant-colonel in 1783 and transferred to the 49th Regiment of Foot in 1790. He was appointed as an aide-de-camp to King George III in 1793, but died on November 18 that year while serving with his regiment on St. Domingo Island (Dansey 2010: 4–5).

A portrait of Lieutenant Colonel Tench Tilghman, one of Washington's aides-de-camp. Tilghman witnessed the fighting at Harlem Heights at first hand. (Hulton Archive/ Getty Images)

Reed watched as the riflemen and rangers "mounted up the Rocks & attacked them [the light infantry]" (quoted in Johnston 1897: 135). Leitch was hit early during the fighting, struck by two balls in the torso and then a third moments later. Not long after, Knowlton was also hit and died an hour later. The two casualties give some evidence of the accuracy of the light infantry's fire. The engagement continued, but the light infantry had been outflanked and were outnumbered. According to Lieutenant Colonel Tench Tilghman, the Patriots initially sent forward as a distraction "gave two fires and then rushed right forward which drove the enemy from the wood and into a Buckwheat field" (quoted in Johnston 1897: 177). The time was around midday.

In the buckwheat field it was the light infantry's chance to be reinforced. Alerted by the musketry audible that morning, the local British commander, Brigadier-General Alexander Leslie, had likewise sent forward reinforcements. The entirety of the 2nd and 3rd Light battalions came to the assistance of their overextended companies, and were joined initially by the Highlanders of the 42nd Foot and some Hessian *Jäger* riflemen. They made a stand in the buckwheat field, where the Patriot forces advanced to meet them.

"Each Party sent in more Succours so that at last it became a very considerable Engagement & Men fell on every side," according to Reed (quoted in Johnston 1897: 135). While the British had been reinforced, so had the Patriots; but Washington had acted more quickly and decisively, and while Crown Forces troops were still being fed into the engagement the Patriots were able to bring to bear a force totaling around 1,800 men. For the next two

Andrew Leitch

Andrew Leitch was born on December 20, 1747, in Lanarkshire, Scotland, and at an unknown date moved to Maryland, and then Virginia. He worked as a merchant and owned a number of indentured servants and slaves. Establishing himself and his family in Dumfries, Virginia, he was accepted within the Virginia planter class and was known to have dined with George Washington at least once, as well as Founding Father and Virginia statesman Patrick Henry.

On February 6, 1776, Leitch was commissioned a lieutenant in the 3rd Virginia Regiment, one of the first Continental Army regiments raised in the state. He aided recruitment efforts prior to joining the main body of the regiment. He was quickly promoted to the rank of major in the 1st Virginia Regiment, but marched with the 3rd Virginia Regiment for New York that spring as that unit was set to arrive under Washington's command sooner.

On September 17, 1776, Leitch was given command of the 3rd Virginia Regiment's rifle companies and tasked with accompanying Knowlton's Rangers in their flanking attack on the British light infantry. While Knowlton was Leitch's superior, the pair seem to have exercised command side-by-side; subsequent accounts of the action, and the commendations of fellow-officers, praised the efforts of both equally, though Washington made particular note of Leitch, who was described as having gallantly led his riflemen in the thickest of the action. The major brought his men into combat and succeeded in driving back the light infantry, though during the fighting he was hit by three separate shots. Carried to the rear, it was initially hoped that he might survive. He was moved to Hackensack Bridge, where he was struck by seizures and lockjaw before dying on September 28. As with Knowlton, his passing was viewed as the loss of a very able officer.

hours the two sides exchanged fire in the buckwheat field. The rangers and riflemen were posted on the left of the Patriot line, where the latter's firepower would have proven especially useful, given that the engagement appears to have occurred at extreme range. Captain Dansey described the action as long and intense (Dansey 2010: 17).

The British fed in yet more reinforcements – grenadier battalions and the 33rd Foot – but they were unable to arrive and deploy in time to stop the original force of light infantry and Highlanders being driven from the buckwheat field. The Continentals pressed them back to the orchard north of the Jones farmhouse, where the 42nd Foot attempted to rally, but the Highlanders' resistance was only momentary. They were again driven back.

At this point the Continental Army forces halted. Reed wrote of how "Our Troops still press'd on drove the Enemy above a Mile & a half till the General ordered them to give over the Pursuit fearing the whole of the Enemy's Army would advance upon them" (quoted in Johnston 1897: 135). By this point the British had been pushed back almost to their own lines and were at last able to mass superior numbers. Conversely, the Continentals' advance had carried the Patriots far from the protection of their own defenses. It was thought prudent to withdraw before a British counterattack risked bringing on a general engagement. The Continentals gave a cheer and marched back to their lines in good order, having held the field.

The British dismissed the engagement at Harlem Heights as a mere affair of outposts. One British officer claimed that the light infantry had put their enemies to the bayonet, and that after the battle the Patriots had paraded three of their own cannons through their encampment claiming

Pictured here as a major-general later in his career, Brigadier-General Alexander Leslie was the commander of the Crown Forces located nearest the initial engagement between light-infantry pickets and Knowlton's Rangers at the battle of Harlem Heights. He was responsible for feeding reinforcements into the developing battle throughout the day, including two of the army's three light-infantry battalions. (Smith Collection/Gado/Getty Images)

A portrait of Colonel Joseph Reed. Also an aide-de-camp to Washington, Reed was present as the Continental Army's commander-in-chief formulated a response to the British light-infantry attack not long after the start of the battle of Harlem Heights. Reed then helped to guide Knowlton's Rangers and the Virginia riflemen in what became their flanking attack. (Smith Collection/Gado/Getty Images)

they had been taken from the British (Nelson 2005: 48). Howe reported back to London that "the light infantry and 42nd regiment with the assistance of the chasseurs [*Jäger*] and field pieces repulsed the enemy with considerable loss" (quoted in Johnston 1897: 204). Captain William Evelyn of the 4th Regiment of Foot, serving with the light infantry, stated that the skirmish "answered no other end than to prove our superiority even in their beloved woods" (quoted in Johnston 1897: 214). The light infantry certainly didn't believe they had been beaten.

On a strategic level, the battle of Harlem Heights was indeed inconsequential. After being outflanked once again in October, Washington abandoned his defenses on Manhattan Island and withdrew farther north, to White Plains. Such an interpretation, however, fails to take into account the impact that the action at Harlem Heights had on Patriot morale. After a month of retreating, the fact that Continental troops had gone toe-to-toe with British light infantry and not only driven them back but held the field at the end of the skirmish meant that the mood of Washington's men improved significantly. Reed observed that "I assure you it has given another Face of Things in our Army – the Men have recovered their Spirits & feel a Confidence which before they had quite lost" (quoted in Johnston 1897: 135). Colonel David Griffith, chaplain and surgeon in the 3rd Virginia Regiment, noted the change in mood, writing that "this affair, tho' not great in itself, is of consequence as it gives spirits to the army, which they wanted. Indeed the confusion was such on Sunday that everybody looked dispirited. At present everything wears a different face" (quoted in Johnston 1897: 172). Tilghman witnessed the shock the British experienced at being attacked by the hitherto cautious Patriots, claiming that "the prisoners we took, told us, they expected our Men would have run away as they did the day before, but that they were never more surprised than to see us advancing to attack them" (quoted in Johnston 1897: 177).

News of the stand made, particularly by the rangers and the riflemen, spread through the Continental Army, helping to convince the Patriots that the enemy could be beaten. The Virginian riflemen in particular were singled out for praise. Tilghman claimed that "the Virginia and Maryland Troops bear the Palm. They are well officered and behave with as much regularity as possible" (quoted in Johnston 1897: 177). Brown observed that the riflemen "got Gen. Washington's thanks yesterday in Publick orders … When Leitch attacked them they retreated from us and we took the ground they occupied. The wood they lay in were cut to pieces by our balls" (quoted in Johnston 1897: 120). Washington did indeed write the day after the engagement praising the efforts of the riflemen, declaring "the General most heartily thanks the troop commanded yesterday by Major Leitch, who first advanced upon the enemy, and the officer who so resolutely supported them" (quoted in Johnston 1897: 162). Griffith wrote of Leitch "he conducted himself on this occasion in a manner that does him the greatest honor, and so did all of his party" (quoted in Johnston 1897: 172). As for Leitch himself, it was thought at first that, despite having been hit by three musket balls, he would survive. His condition worsened unexpectedly, however, and he died 12 days after the battle.

OPPOSITE
This map, sketched by a British officer possibly just after the fighting at Harlem Heights, gives a good basic view of the battlefield, as well as the initial entrenchments out of which both sides operated. The Hudson River runs between the upper and lower edges of the map, with the Hollow Way on the right (eastern) side of the river and the Morningside Heights immediately due south of the Hollow Way. (Library of Congress)

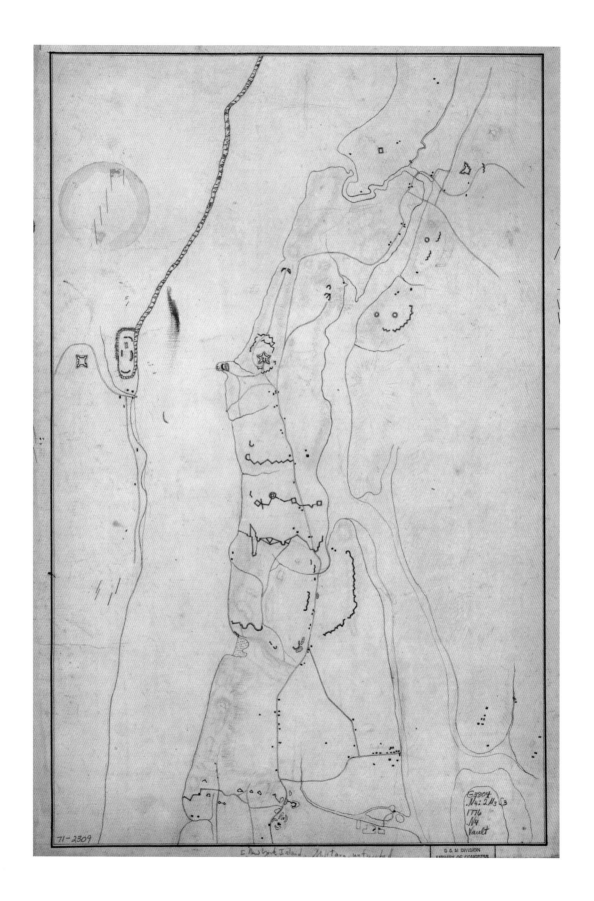

C. New York Island   Military unfinished

Freeman's Farm

September 19, 1777

BACKGROUND TO BATTLE

In June 1777 a Crown Forces army under the command of Major-General John Burgoyne marched south from Canada with the strategic objective of seizing control of the Hudson River and, in tandem with Howe's capture of New York the year before, cutting off the seat of the rebellion in New England from the

Pictured here in an illustration from 1778, Brigadier-General Simon Fraser commanded the Crown Forces' Advance Corps during the Saratoga campaign, including the precious composite battalion of light infantry. Fraser was an active and well-liked officer, admired for his spirit and alacrity, and his death at the battle of Bemis Heights was met with much mourning. (Sepia Times/ Universal Images Group via Getty Images)

middle colonies. Initially, the campaign went well for the Crown Forces. The British captured what was considered a vital fortress at Ticonderoga, New York, on July 6, but the logistical difficulties associated with campaigning in what was essentially the interior wilderness slowed the expedition down. There was a further setback when a foraging force of Braunschweig dragoons and Loyalists were defeated at the battle of Bennington on August 16. Dissatisfied with the campaign and alienated by Burgoyne, the First Nations forces allied to the expedition abandoned it. With winter approaching, Burgoyne chose to press on rather than go into quarters at Ticonderoga. Abandoning his posts farther north, his army crossed the Hudson near the settlement of Saratoga, New York, completing the passage on September 15.

Meanwhile, the situation of the Patriot army opposing Burgoyne had been steadily improving since the loss of Ticonderoga. Major General Horatio Gates took command of Continental Army forces on August 19, and his army swelled with both local militia and Continental reinforcements sent north by Washington. The Patriots secured a strong defensive position at Bemis Heights, roughly 10 miles south of Saratoga. The road farther south passed through a narrow defile, penned between the Hudson and the Bemis Heights. Patriot forces began digging in, siting timber redoubts that the British would be forced to storm if they wished to continue moving south.

After crossing the Hudson Burgoyne's forces began to push south and discovered the Patriot defenses blocking their progress. While Gates had fortified much of Bemis Heights, the most elevated position, on the Patriot left, remained unoccupied. These bluffs, though steep and thickly forested, if taken would command the Patriot fortifications lower down and allow for a flanking maneuver. Aware of this, Gates permitted Major General Benedict Arnold to take a portion of the Patriot army and advance north beyond the fortifications on Bemis Heights, meeting the British head-on and intercepting them before they could turn the Patriot left.

Burgoyne's expedition included a single light-infantry battalion, a composite force consisting of the light companies of the 9th, 20th, 21st, 24th, 29th, 31st, 34th, 47th, 53rd, and 62nd regiments of Foot. These troops had some experience of campaigning in Canada in 1776, and had further trained under Burgoyne ahead of the 1777 expedition. Indeed, in preparation for a campaign in the wilderness Burgoyne had inculcated the light-infantry ethos throughout his entire army. The uniforms had been modified in line with those of the light troops to be more practical in forested terrain, and the regulars – even the German troops – had been practicing styles of combat in keeping with the woodland skirmishing that would be expected of them. The light infantry were also taught new exercises described as assisting their effectiveness in forest fighting, with the whole battalion utilizing the rare opportunity of having all their companies collected together in order to practice for the expected campaign (Hubner 1986: 91).

Burgoyne's expedition was initially well supported by First Nations allies, who provided valuable assistance in scouting and irregular warfare. Supplementing these forces was a company of about 50 men drawn from the line regiments and commanded by Captain Alexander Fraser. Known as Fraser's Rangers or the Company of Select Marksmen, these picked soldiers performed duties similar to both the light infantry and the irregulars. After the First Nations contingent largely melted away prior to the battle of Freeman's Farm, the actions of these light troops became even more vital to Burgoyne's operations.

As part of the Continental reinforcements he had sent north, Washington had released the recently formed rifle corps commanded by Colonel Morgan. This force was an amalgamation of men from many of the rifle companies raised earlier in the American Revolutionary War, as well as soldiers and officers personally picked by Morgan. Their work contesting the British advance in New Jersey in early 1777 was praised by Continental Army Colonel Henry Knox, who wrote that "we had a large body of riflemen, under Colonel Morgan, perpetually making inroads upon them, attacking their pickets, killing their

A depiction of Benedict Arnold. The most high-profile Continental Army defector of the American Revolutionary War, Arnold rose to the rank of major general in the Continental Army before defecting to the British in 1780. His presence at the battle of Freeman's Farm remains contested – seemingly he gave directions to Morgan and his riflemen at the start of the action, but was absent for most of it, conferring with Major General Horatio Gates at Bemis Heights. (Stock Montage/Getty Images)

light-horse," and went on to describe them as "the most respectable body of continental troops that ever were in America" (Knox 1873: 45). Regarding sending them north, Washington wrote that "the people in the Northern Army seem so intimidated by the Indians that I have determined to send up Colo. Morgan's Corps of Rifle Men who will fight them in their own way" (Washington 1939: 70). In another letter he described the riflemen as "all chosen Men Selected from the Army at large; well acquainted with, the use of Rifles and with that mode of Fighting, which is Necessary to make them a good Counterpoise to the Indians, and have distinguished themselves on a variety of occasions Since the formation of the Corps, in Skirmishes with the Enemy" (Washington 1939: 78).

A portrait of Lieutenant Colonel Richard Butler. Born in 1743, Butler was an officer in the Continental Army and second-in-command of Morgan's rifle corps. A friend of Morgan's, he was present commanding the riflemen at the battles of Saratoga; he went on to command the 9th Pennsylvania Regiment. Butler was killed in action on November 4, 1791, during the battle of the Wabash, at which the US Army was decisively defeated by First Nations warriors of the Western Confederacy. (Kean Collection/Getty Images)

When the riflemen arrived they were brigaded by Gates with Colonel Henry Dearborn's battalion of light infantry. This unit of smoothbore-armed skirmishers had been formed as a direct copy of the British practice of assembling composite light-infantry battalions. Much like Morgan's riflemen, the men were chosen from Continental Army regiments and drawn together to form a battalion approximately 300 strong. With the arrival of Morgan it was realized that the light infantry would provide ideal companions for the riflemen. Armed with bayonets, the light infantrymen could give the vital close combat support necessary to shield the vulnerable riflemen without hampering their skirmishing capabilities. They were therefore brigaded together into a 694-strong corps, viewed as the elite of the Patriot army in the north. At the time of the battle, however, they had been employed together for only eight days, and the combined corps' lack of combat experience was betrayed by some weaknesses when the fighting started.

Burgoyne decided to divide his army into three main columns and probe toward the Patriot lines on Bemis Heights, likely hoping that the right-hand column in particular would be able to secure the high ground on the Patriot left. While the left-hand column consisted mostly of the German troops and the central column of the line regiments, the light-infantry battalion was with the right-hand column, commanded by Brigadier-General Simon Fraser, an experienced leader of light infantry. Because the light companies were all concentrated together, and due to the fact that most of the First Nations allied warriors had abandoned the British cause by this point, companies were detached from the regular battalions to act as an advance party for the central column. Fraser's Rangers and the remaining First Nations allies formed the vanguard of the right-hand column. The British set out at dawn, initially in a morning fog that quickly burned off. On the Patriot side, Arnold sent forward a vanguard comprised of the Continental Army light infantry and Morgan's rifle corps.

MAP KEY

1 *c.***1215hrs:** British pickets walk into the clearing around Freeman's Farm and are engaged by Patriot riflemen and light infantry already occupying the buildings. The pickets are driven back.

2 *c.***1230hrs:** The Patriot riflemen charge the withdrawing pickets, losing unit cohesion as they do so.

3 *c.***1235hrs:** The rest of the Crown Forces column the pickets are screening begins to move up to the tree line and engages the riflemen.

4 *c.***1245hrs:** Two British light-infantry companies and one artillery piece sent from the Advance Corps catch the scattered riflemen in the flank, routing them.

5 *c.***1300hrs:** The light companies return to the light battalion with the Advance Corps. As the action becomes a general engagement they remain only lightly engaged on the British right flank.

6 *c.***1330hrs:** Morgan is able to rally his riflemen. They spend the rest of the engagement dispersed, targeting the British at range.

Battlefield environment

The engagement centered around a farm belonging to Loyalist John Freeman, who may have acted as a guide for Burgoyne's forces. It consisted of several log houses or cabins at the center of a clearing. This space contained felled trees, tree-stumps, and weeds, and was around 385yd by 165yd. It was surrounded by a rail fence (Hubner 1986: 126). On the British side of the clearing was a ravine. The woodland surrounding the clearing was dense, consisting largely of oaks, maples, and white pine (Ketchum 1997: 360). Besides a few other nearby clearings, the battlefield was further hemmed in to the east by the Hudson River. The main Patriot defenses on Bemis Heights lay about 1½ miles south of Freeman's Farm.

Even by the standards of North American battlefields, the terrain was particularly broken and difficult to traverse. Burgoyne's decision to divide his army into three columns, while understandable given the limited usability of the tracks leading through the surrounding forests, ensured that communication and support between his army's sections would be hampered, especially for the leftmost column, consisting mostly of the German troops, who were at a greater distance from the central and right-hand columns. Conversely, the forested terrain offered ample opportunity for the light troops on both sides to fight in the style for which they were best known. How effectively they would be employed by their respective commanders was another matter.

An artillery piece not dissimilar to the one that operated alongside British light infantry at the opening of the battle of Freeman's Farm. Coordination between different units and arms was an important aspect of tactics with which the Patriots initially struggled. The former location of Freeman's Farm itself is out of view to the right of the image. (Jiayin Ma/ Moment Open/Getty Images)

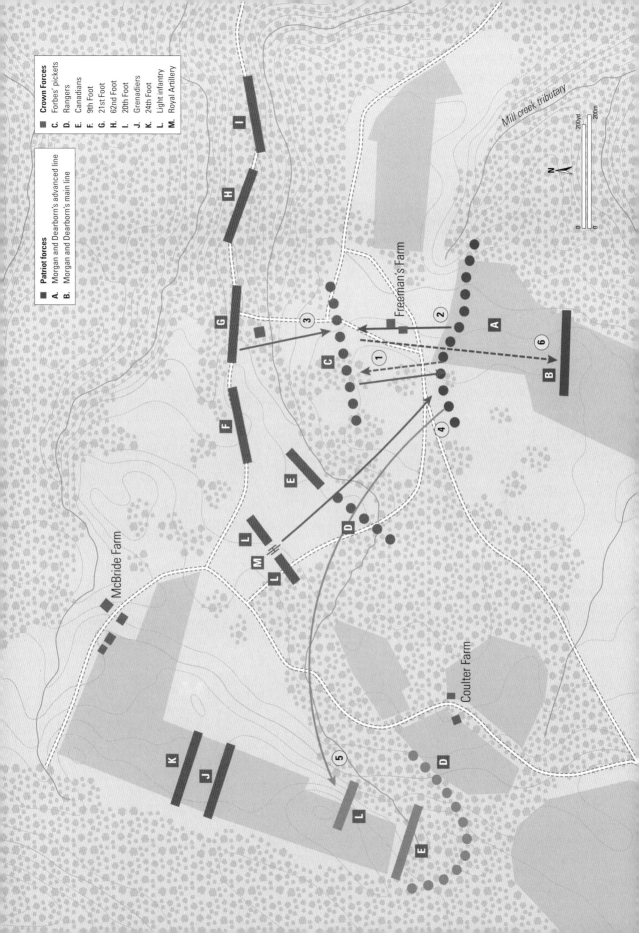

Patriot forces
■ **A.** Morgan and Dearborn's advanced line
■ **B.** Morgan and Dearborn's main line

Crown Forces
■ **C.** Forbes' pickets
D. Rangers
E. Canadians
F. 9th Foot
G. 21st Foot
H. 62nd Foot
I. 20th Foot
J. Grenadiers
K. 24th Foot
L. Light infantry
M. Royal Artillery

N

200yd
200m

Mill creek tributary

Freeman's Farm

McBride Farm

Coulter Farm

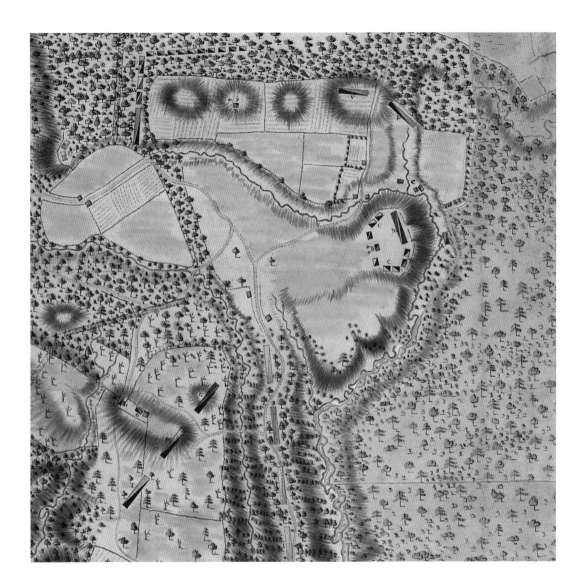

This detail from a British map published in 1777 shows various positions of the British forces, including the light-infantry battalion, during the battle of Freeman's Farm. The overview shows the overall British dispositions, with the dotted edges and paler colors denoting the initial positions of the various units and the solid edges and stronger colors their second positions. (Library of Congress)

INTO COMBAT

John Freeman's farm lay between the two advancing forces. The Patriot vanguard reached it first, with at least two companies of riflemen occupying the log buildings, rail fences, and the trees on their side of the clearing.

It wasn't long before the central British column also arrived. The picked companies drawn from the 9th, 20th, 21st, and 62nd regiments of Foot, a force totaling approximately 100 men, had been placed under the command of Major Gordon Forbes. For the purpose of scouting ahead, these companies were essentially employed as light infantry, a tactic aided by the fact that Burgoyne had pushed for light-infantry-style uniforms and doctrine to be adopted by his entire force.

The vanguard emerged into the clearing where Freeman's Farm was located amid only light firing, seemingly unaware of the size of the Patriot force lying in wait for them at what a British officer described as "a house and some fences" (Burgoyne 1780: 69). Captain Ezekiel Wakefield of Dearborn's light

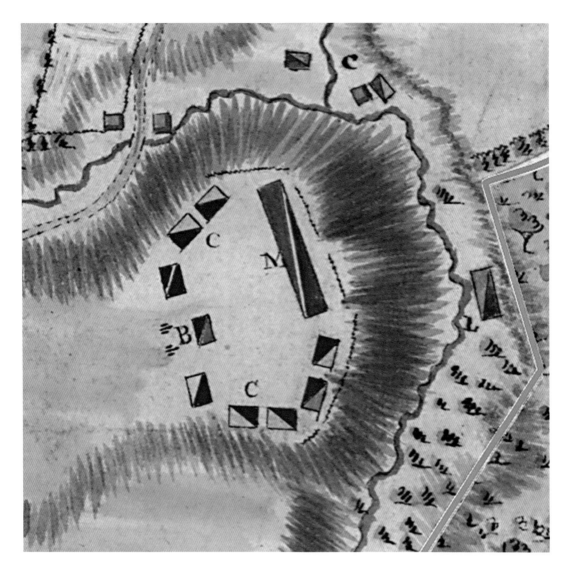

infantry recalled that Arnold (whose actual presence for much of the battle was nebulous) was with Morgan at the time, and "pointing to the enemy emerging from the woods into an opening partially cleared, covered with stumps and fallen timber, addressing Morgan, he said … let your riflemen cure them of their borrowed plumes" (Wakefield 1880: 311). The Patriot riflemen let the British close the distance before delivering a devastatingly accurate volley as close range. Lieutenant William Digby of the 53rd Foot's grenadier company described the Patriots as having "greater superiority of fire" and wrote of "every officer being either killed or wounded except one" (quoted in Baxter 1887: 272). Forbes himself was wounded and the pickets devastated in the brief exchange. The commander of the Patriot light infantry, Dearborn, wrote that "the Rifle and Light Infantry Corps turned out to meet the enemy and about 2 miles from our camp we fell in with their advance guard and attacked them" (Dearborn 1939: 105).

The British pickets were driven back. At the same time, Fraser heard the sounds of musketry coming from his left. Aware that the central column,

This detail from the 1777 map shows the dispositions of the Crown Forces artillery and light troops in the northern part of the battlefield, including the Royal Artillery detachment (**B**), the various British light-infantry companies (**C**), the Braunschweig *Jäger* company (**L**), and the Braunschweig *chasseur* battalion (**M**). (Library of Congress)

Freeman's Farm

Patriot view: Colonel Morgan's riflemen initially surprised and routed British pickets after they had entered the clearing around the occupied farm. Overconfident, the riflemen have charged the British skirmishers despite their lack of bayonets, driving the damaged British vanguard back toward the woods from which they had initially advanced. Morgan's riflemen have failed, however, to anticipate the arrival of the main British column through the forest after their advance guards. While the redcoats rally at the tree line, an even greater problem develops for Morgan's men. Several light-infantry companies supported by light artillery have been dispatched from the British right and have now caught them in the left flank while they are still exposed in the clearing. Under fire from both cannons and muskets from front and side, the disorganized riflemen lack the support of bayonet-armed infantry, and are beginning to break and rout. They will later re-form under Morgan's command, however, and play an important role in the general engagement that unfolds throughout the day.

British view: These soldiers of the light-infantry company of the 21st Foot are engaging the flank of overextended companies from Morgan's rifle corps. They have been dispatched to assist the vanguard of the British column that has run into trouble at Freeman's Farm. Along with the 21st Foot personnel is a Royal Artillery 3-pdr cannon and the light company of the 24th Foot, farther to the right of the cannon. All are from Brigadier-General Fraser's Advance Corps, the main body of which remains on the British right flank. The light infantry are firing and advancing by files over the tree-stumps and weeds filling the clearing around the farm of John Freeman, utilizing extended order, which allows them to skirmish effectively on the broken ground. As they do so, they operate in close support with the artillery, which guarantees them superior range and weight of fire over the enemy.

which was the smallest of the three prongs, might need support, he detached two light-infantry companies from the composite battalion along with one or two artillery pieces and possibly two companies of the 24th Foot (sources differ slightly). Fraser's Rangers may also have supplemented the relief effort. This corps of around 150–200 men was sent eastward toward the sounds of the developing meeting engagement.

The defeat of the pickets led to a surge of aggression from the Patriot light infantry and riflemen. Seeing the redcoat skirmishers beginning to run back toward the woodland from which they had emerged, the Patriots charged. This movement included the riflemen, despite their lack of bayonets. Unfortunately, however, the main body of the central column had come up through the forest in support of their vanguard. As the Patriots closed the distance, they realized too late that the woods were occupied by four battalions of British infantry advancing to meet them. As they opened fire, some of the pickets still scrambling to get out of the clearing were hit by their own side.

It was now the riflemen's turn to be out of position and exposed. The impetuosity of their charge displayed either indiscipline, or overconfidence among the officers. To make matters worse, British light infantry now came up on the left flank of Morgan's corps. In their usual style, they engaged as skirmishers, moving forward in pairs and firing by files, one man taking aim and discharging while his partner loaded. To this brisk fire was added that of the 3-pdr cannon supporting them, likely using grapeshot against the dispersed Patriots (Snow 2016: 99).

This use of combined arms was in contrast to the situation in which the Patriots found themselves. While the combination of bayonet-wielding light infantry with riflemen could have made for an excellent fighting force, circumstances had left the riflemen scattered and unsupported. The situation grew worse as the British pressed their advantage and all unit-wide cohesion was lost among the Patriots. Flight ensued, with the Patriot riflemen retreating back across the clearing to Freeman's Farm and then farther to the woodland beyond. Dearborn wrote that "after fighting about half an hour being overpowered with numbers we were obliged to retire to a height, about 50 rods [approximately 270yd] and there were reinforced" (Dearborn 1939: 106). Digby likewise recalled that "the line came up to their support and obliged Morgan in his turn to retreat with loss" (quoted in Baxter 1887: 272). The engagement had lasted about a half-hour. The clearing with Freeman's Farm in the center was left as a no man's land between the two sides, the buildings "almost encircled with dead" (Wilkinson 1816: 237).

It seemed as though Morgan's corps had been severely attrited. A Patriot officer, Lieutenant Colonel James Wilkinson, had ridden on his own initiative from the main encampment at Bemis Heights when he heard the first of the firing, and arrived just after the Patriot withdrawal from the farm. After first finding a small party of the Patriot light infantry rallying under their officers, he came across Morgan's second-in-command, Lieutenant Colonel Richard Butler, who had only three men with him still, all sheltering behind trees. Butler related the midday encounter: "that having forced the picket, they had closed with the British line, had been instantly routed, and from the suddenness of the shock and the broken nature of the ground, were broken and scattered in all directions" (quoted in Wilkinson 1816: 237). Butler also stated that it was not only Patriot riflemen who were marksmen – he warned Wilkinson about "the enemy's sharpshooters," saying that "being on horseback, I should attract a shot" (quoted in Wilkinson 1816: 237). There had indeed been a number of casualties among the Patriot officers during the initial engagement.

Wilkinson then encountered Morgan himself. The effects of the sharp skirmish around the farm seemed to have momentarily broken the rifle officer. Wilkinson recalled that he "perceived Colonel Morgan attended by two men only, who with a turkey call, was collecting his dispersed troops. The moment I came up to him, he burst into tears, and exclaimed 'I am ruined, by G-d! ... my men are scattered God knows where'" (Wilkinson 1816: 238). According to Wilkinson's account, Morgan had missed the foremost fighting at the farm due to the fact he had been ensuring the rearmost section of his corps entered the engagement, and by the time he reached the front the situation had already deteriorated. Wilkinson informed Morgan "that he had a long day before him to retrieve an inauspicious beginning, and informed him where I had seen his field officers, which appeared to cheer him" (Wilkinson 1816: 237).

The lull in the fighting continued. Morgan, "Partly from discipline, and partly from the directing sounds of the turkey call," was able to re-form his corps seemingly almost in its entirely (Graham 1856: 145–46). This spoke to the spirit and determination of the riflemen, confirming the high regard in which they were held within the Continental Army. They would make an important contribution during the rest of the engagement.

The British light infantry, meanwhile, had halted as part of Fraser's column. Burgoyne decided to press the attack on the Patriots as they amassed in the woods across from Freeman's Farm. Around 1400hrs his central column was ordered forward. Meanwhile Fraser's Advance Corps, including the light infantry, were posted on a low hill on the British right flank, about 260yd from the reserve regiment. Here their purpose was that of a holding force.

By 1500hrs the central column was heavily engaged. Morgan's riflemen, re-formed, were put to use as the fighting swung back and forth around Freeman's Farm. Their firing contributed to the heavy casualties sustained, particularly among the officers of the central column. Sergeant Roger Lamb wrote that "several of the Americans placed themselves in high trees, and, as often as they could distinguish a British officer's uniform, took him off by deliberately aiming at his person" (quoted in Frost 1848: 150). Lamb's general description gives a good indication of the ferocity of the fighting:

A constant blaze of fire was kept up, and both armies seemed to be determined on death or victory. The Americans and British alternately drove, and were driven, by each other. Men, and particularly officers, dropped every moment and on every side ... Few actions have been characterized by more obstinacy in attack or defence. The British repeatedly tried their bayonets, but without their usual success in the use of that weapon. (Quoted in Frost 1848: 150)

OPPOSITE
An example of the .75-caliber 1769 Short Land Pattern smoothbore flintlock musket. It was standard issue to British light infantry during the American Revolutionary War. Reasonably durable and effective at ranges up to 200yd, it was a formidable weapon in the right hands. In most engagements Patriot officers suffered as many casualties as their British counterparts, and British commanders noted that when used by experienced soldiers such as those in the light companies the Short Land Pattern was an effective small arm. (Fotosearch/Getty Images)

Burgoyne also later paid tribute to the deadly effectiveness of Morgan's riflemen, noting that:

> The enemy had with their great numbers of marksmen, armed with rifle-barrel pieces: these, during an engagement, hovered upon the flanks in small detachments, and were very expert in securing themselves, and in shifting their ground. In this action, many placed themselves in high trees in the rear of their own line, and there was seldom a minute's interval of smoke, in any part of our line without officers being taken off by a single shot. (Burgoyne 1780: 163)

The riflemen did not only target officers, but also the Royal Artillery crewmen working the cannons supporting the British line. In total 36 of the 48 personnel operating the artillery pieces were killed or wounded over the course of the action. This allowed the Patriots to charge and overrun the artillery pieces on several occasions, though they were driven back by British counterattacks. In all about half the troops of the central column were killed or wounded during the sustained firefight. One British officer, Thomas Anburey, recalled how "our army … abounded with young officers, in the subaltern line, and in the course of this unpleasant duty [the burial of the dead] three of the 20th regiment were interred together, the age of the eldest not exceeding seventeen" (quoted in Baxter 1887: 272).

All the while the British light infantry remained largely static on their hill. Only at one point did they move briefly to support the center, and on two other occasions drove off attacks by the Patriot left. Fraser's Rangers seem to have acted as the screen protecting the extreme right of the British line, as they suffered the heaviest casualties among the right-hand column, losing 40 percent of their strength as they skirmished with the advancing Patriots. The hill they were occupying, however, constituted the British flank – leaving it under-defended could have offered an opportunity to the Patriots to turn Burgoyne's outnumbered army. Further considerations likely stayed Burgoyne's hand. As far as he was concerned, the fighting around Freeman's Farm wasn't a general engagement, but a prelude to his attack on the Patriot positions farther south, on Bemis Heights. Anticipating a hard-fought future engagement and the likelihood of having to storm entrenched Patriot defenses, Burgoyne probably wished to avoid heavy casualties among his elite troops, keeping them fresh for what he hoped would be the decisive battle in the coming days. Because of this, after the initial, indecisive defeat of Morgan's riflemen, the British light infantry played only a minor role in the battle of Freeman's Farm. Burgoyne's caution with his elite troops may have contributed to heavier losses among the line infantry, but strategically there was little the light infantry could do to improve their commander's chances of victory.

The fighting was decided when the third of Burgoyne's columns, consisting of German troops mostly from Braunschweig, arrived on the Patriot right. Morgan's riflemen were among the first engaged, and a fighting withdrawal was conducted as the Patriots pulled back toward Bemis Heights, leaving the Crown Forces in control of the field as the sun set. Toward the end of the battle Patriot forces came close to turning

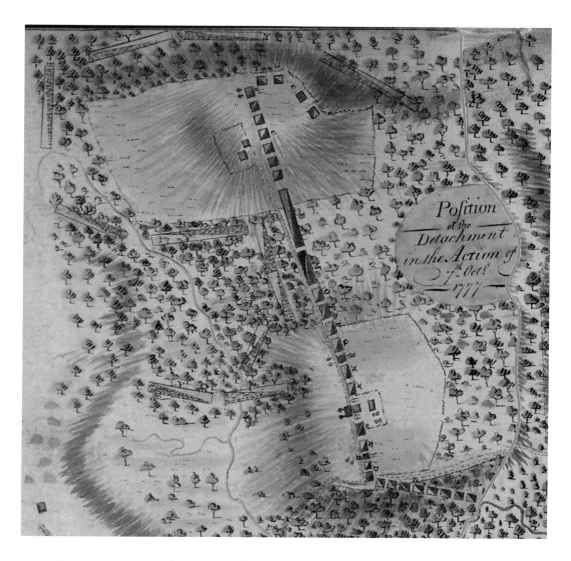

Position
of the
Detachment
in the Action of
7th Octr
1777

This detail from the 1777 map featured earlier (see pages 48 and 49) shows the British dispositions at the battle of Bemis Heights, with the British artillery (**B**) and the British light infantry (**C**) anchoring the western end of the Crown Forces battle line. (Library of Congress)

the flank of the 62nd Foot, which had been heavily engaged throughout the combat. A Royal Artillery officer, Second Lieutenant James Murray Hadden, reported that "During the attack on the 62nd Regt. two companies of light were advanced on our left and effectually cleared us of any attack which was not renewed "till they were withdrawn" (quoted in Hubner 1986: 129). Wilkinson likewise reported that late on, a Patriot brigade did get "into action with part of the British light corps ... and of consequence they were but lightly engaged, as is manifest from their losses" (Wilkinson 1816: 239). This seems to have been the only time after the initial engagement that a portion of the light battalion sallied forth from their hill.

Tactically, the battle of Freeman's Farm was another largely indecisive engagement, but it stalled the British advance. The Patriots withdrew back to their lines on Bemis Heights while Burgoyne dug in on the edge of the clearing that had seen so much bloodshed. The British commander initially intended to follow up immediately with his grenadier and light battalions, but decided the line troops were too exhausted. He soon

received news that Major General Henry Clinton was intending to move from New York to support him, causing him to delay further. The wait was to prove in vain, however – Clinton failed to link up with Burgoyne, leaving him essentially stranded. Burgoyne attempted to break out by attacking Bemis Heights on October 7, where he was defeated. Morgan's riflemen again proved their worth, while the British light infantry covered the British withdrawal after initial defeat, then stubbornly defended a redoubt from repeated Patriot attacks. In the aftermath the British withdrew north but, finding the route back up the Hudson River blocked by more Patriot forces, Burgoyne was left with no choice other than to surrender at Saratoga on October 17, 1777.

This painting by John Trumbull (1756–1843) shows Burgoyne surrendering his army to Gates near Saratoga, New York, on October 17, 1777. Visible alongside the Continental commander is Colonel Daniel Morgan, wearing his iconic hunting shirt, completed with a crimson officer's sash. Morgan's riflemen contributed effectively to the Patriot victory. (John Parrot/Stocktrek Images/Getty Images)

This illustration depicts the prison camp for Burgoyne's army at Charlottesville, Virginia. Along with the rest of Burgoyne's army, the light-infantry companies marched into captivity. Escape and desertion were widespread, however, and some prisoners made it back to British lines as the war progressed. (Encyclopaedia Britannica/UIG Via Getty Images)

Hanging Rock

August 6, 1780

BACKGROUND TO BATTLE

On May 12, 1780, Charleston, the largest settlement in South Carolina and one of the chief ports on the Eastern Seaboard, surrendered to the besieging Crown Forces. As part of their efforts to shift the war into the southern colonies and, hopefully, attract more Loyalists to their cause, the British established a series of outposts throughout South Carolina in the summer of 1780. Several of these were sited along the Catawba River valley, the largest of which were the posts at Rocky Mount and, farther north, Hanging Rock. The latter sat astride the road between the settlements of Charlotte and Camden.

During the same period, Patriot resistance was being organized largely around groups of militia and partisans. One of the leading figures in the Continental Army following the defeat at Charleston in May 1780 was Colonel Thomas Sumter, who took control of various militia forces and conducted a series of raids designed to undermine the newly established British control of South Carolina. On July 30, Sumter launched an attack on the Rocky Mount outpost. In order to keep forces at neighboring Hanging Rock occupied, he sent a diversionary force under Major William Richardson Davie to attack that outpost at the same time.

Davie's force consisted of 40 dragoons and 40 mounted riflemen. They fell upon three companies of Loyalists belonging to the North Carolina Royalists, encamped close to – but separate from – Hanging Rock's main garrison. The surprise was total. Davie described how "the rifle company, under Captain [Samuel] Flenchaw, passed the camp sentries without being challenged, dismounted in the lane, and gave the enemy a well directed fire" (Davie 1848: 23). After this the confused Loyalists "were surrounded by the dragoons who had entered the field, and were literally cut to pieces. All this

was done under the eye of the whole British camp, so that no prisoners could be safely taken. This may account for, and possibly excuse, the slaughter that took place" (Davie 1848: 23). The Patriots snatched horses and muskets from the defeated Loyalists and made good their escape before the main camp could respond.

The raid against Hanging Rock went better for the Patriots than the main attack on Rocky Mount. Sumter was forced to retreat during a rainstorm and in the aftermath he determined to launch his main force against Hanging Rock. The decision was unwittingly abetted by the local Crown Forces, who shifted troops from Hanging Rock to Rocky Mount, anticipating that Sumter would attempt to attack the same outpost twice.

Owing to manpower shortages, the Crown Forces defending both positions were Loyalist Americans rather than British regulars. Loyalists were typically organized into two distinct groups: the Provincial Corps, a professional soldiery based on the organization of the British Army; and the more irregular militia. Hanging Rock's defenders were drawn from both groups. Three different Provincial Corps regiments had detachments present – the British Legion, the Prince of Wales's American Volunteers, and the Royal North Carolina Regiment. The British Legion in particular was one of the most effective Loyalist regiments raised during the American Revolutionary War. It was a composite force of dragoons and light infantry; the two companies garrisoning Hanging Rock consisted only of the latter, commanded by Captain Kenneth McCulloch and Captain John Rousselet and totaling 160 men. Bolstering these roughly 500 Provincial Loyalists were 800 Loyalist militiamen, mostly from the Camden district of South Carolina, though they included a detachment that had journeyed from North Carolina.

ABOVE LEFT
This portrait of Colonel Francis Rawdon dates from later in his life. A British officer of Irish origin, Rawdon was given responsibility for Crown control of large areas of the south in 1780 and 1781. He sought to make up for the lack of regular British light infantry in the southern theater by using Loyalist Provincial Corps light troops. (The Print Collector/Print Collector/Getty Images)

ABOVE RIGHT
William Richardson Davie, depicted here much later in life, emigrated from England to North America in 1763. Joining the Patriot militia in 1778, he led mounted militiamen and light dragoons. Davie played a prominent role under Sumter, but fell out with the commander over tactics at Hanging Rock. (Hulton Archive/Getty Images)

A portrait of Thomas Sumter. Born in Virginia in 1734, Sumter was elected as colonel of the 2nd South Carolina Regiment of the Continental Army in 1776. He became a brigadier general on October 6, 1780, and played an important role in resurrecting Patriot resistance in South Carolina. Sumter's partisan efforts were curtailed when he was badly wounded at the battle of Blackstock's Farm on November 20, 1780, but he recovered to pursue a career in politics. He died on June 1, 1832. (Hulton Archive/ Getty Images)

There were also two 3-pdr cannons present, captured from the Patriots in Camden.

Sumter's force consisted of a mixture of militia units totaling around 800 men, including a small force of 35 allied Catawba warriors. The militia regiments carried a mixture of smoothbore and rifled firearms, and many were mounted. Their combat experience was mixed – fighting, almost exclusively against Loyalists, had been occurring on and off since 1776, but by the summer of 1780 had begun to approach fever pitch. The partisan style of warfare practiced by both sides involved traveling fast and light, sometimes with soldiers doubling up on horses. Surprise attacks were preferred, and after a fight the troops usually disengaged quickly and withdrew rather than holding ground, wary of retaliatory strikes.

As part of his plan to attack the Hanging Rock outpost, Sumter divided his force into three columns. One was commanded by Davie, consisting primarily of his own Independent Corps of Light Horse and Major Richard Winn's regiment of militia, as well as assorted volunteers and detached companies. The second column, commanded by Colonel William Hill, was composed primarily of what Davie described as the South Carolina refugees, while the final column, led by Colonel Robert Irwin, was formed of militia

This contemporary image shows a light infantryman and a hussar of the Queen's Rangers. Alongside the British Legion, the Queen's Rangers was among the most effective Loyalist units of the American Revolutionary War. Like the British Legion, the Queen's Rangers were a legion formation, which meant a regiment that included both light cavalry and light infantry – in this case, the cavalry in question were hussars, but usually they were dragoons. The differences were cosmetic. The light infantryman shows the usual black leather accouterments and cap employed by both British regular light infantry and the Loyalist Provincial Corps light infantry. (Courtesy of Toronto Public Library)

from Mecklenburg County (Davie 1848: 26). A reserve force consisting of 60 horsemen and 50 riflemen would follow up on the attack. Davie wished to engage the enemy on foot, worrying that the engagement wouldn't be decided by a single charge and that dismounting and deploying while under fire was difficult. Sumter overruled him.

The Loyalist forces were located in three encampments spread along the road to Camden. Described by Davie as an open camp, the positions included little to nothing in the way of fortifications. The most northwesterly encampment, situated on a small rise, was where the Loyalist militia had based themselves. A little under a half-mile southeast were the Royal North Carolinians and the British Legion's light infantry. The third and final encampment, another half-mile farther southeast, consisted of the Prince of Wales's American Volunteers. Although elements of the Provincials had some prior campaign experience in the northern colonies, overall the state of command at Hanging Rock was not ideal – Major John Carden of the Prince of Wales's American Volunteers had recently been promoted to leadership of the outpost after the previous commanding officer, Lieutenant Colonel Thomas Pattinson, had been found drunk during an inspection by local Crown Forces commander Colonel Francis Rawdon. Morale was also poor after Davie's brutal raid, especially among the Loyalist militia.

MAP KEY

1 *c.*0700hrs: After dividing into three columns the Patriots strike, but the attack is premature, only hitting the most northernly Loyalist camp rather than all three simultaneously. The surprised Loyalist militia are routed from the first camp and flee through the two that lie farther south.

2 *c.*0730hrs: The Patriots carry on and attack the second camp, belonging to various units from the Loyalist Provincial Corps, including light infantry from the British Legion. They mount several counterattacks with bayonets that briefly halt the Patriot advance.

3 *c.*0800hrs: The Loyalist resistance deteriorates and the survivors of the second camp scatter or flee to the final camp farther south. A detachment from the Prince of Wales's American Volunteers, stationed in the final camp, advances and outflanks the Patriots, but the Loyalists are eventually driven back.

4 *c.*0900hrs: The commander of the British outpost, Major John Carden, hands command to his subordinate, Captain John Rousselet of the British Legion light infantry. The remaining Loyalists form a hollow square at the center of the third and final camp. Elements of the Patriot force advance to the tree line and open fire at range.

5 *c.*1200hrs: Unable to close with the hollow square decisively, much of the Patriot militia instead busy themselves with looting the two captured camps. Patriot dragoons charge and disperse a section of Loyalist troops rallying outside of the hollow square.

6 *c.*1230hrs: Mounted Loyalist light infantry of the British Legion arrive from the direction of Rocky Mount, but are dispersed by the Patriot dragoons. Realizing there is a danger of further reinforcements being sent, the Patriots withdraw.

Battlefield environment

The Patriots approached from the north and northwest. The first part of the Hanging Rock outpost they would come into contact with was the Loyalist militia encampment, described by William Dobein James as set upon "a hill side covered with trees"; beyond it was the Charlotte–Camden road, which passed through "a small stream of water" and "a valley covered with brush wood" (James 1829: 90). This valley was described as "a creek with a deep ravine" that appears to have been quite steep and rocky in places (Davie 1848: 25). The hanging rock itself was a large boulder with an overhang that lay north of the arc of encampments. There were also several log houses around which the central encampment had been erected.

Davie reported that the two Provincial encampments had tolerable lines of sight on the approaches: "the position of the regular troops could not be approached without an entire exposure of the assailants" (Davie 1848: 25). This more open ground was bisected in places by fences. There may have also been a stockade to the south of the encampment being used by the Prince of Wales's American Volunteers, though it seems to have played no part in the fighting – some descriptions of the action mention small, crude redoubts, but in general there appears to have been little in the way of defensive works protection the open-plan encampments.

The Patriot forces therefore faced a number of challenges: they would have to either strike the encampments one at a time and hope that surprise and momentum would carry the day; or they could seek to divide their forces, despite being outnumbered, and try to hit the three encampments simultaneously. Sumter decided upon the latter plan. The heat of the day and the fact that Sumter's forces possessed limited ammunition would further impact the ensuing action.

HANGING ROCK, SOUTH CAROLINA.

Dating from the 1860s, this is a rendering of the actual hanging rock after which the battle of August 6, 1780, was named. The large boulder sits in the midst of woodland beside the Charlotte–Camden road. Its overhang provided a degree of shelter from the elements for a small group of men. (Lakeview Images/Alamy Stock Photo)

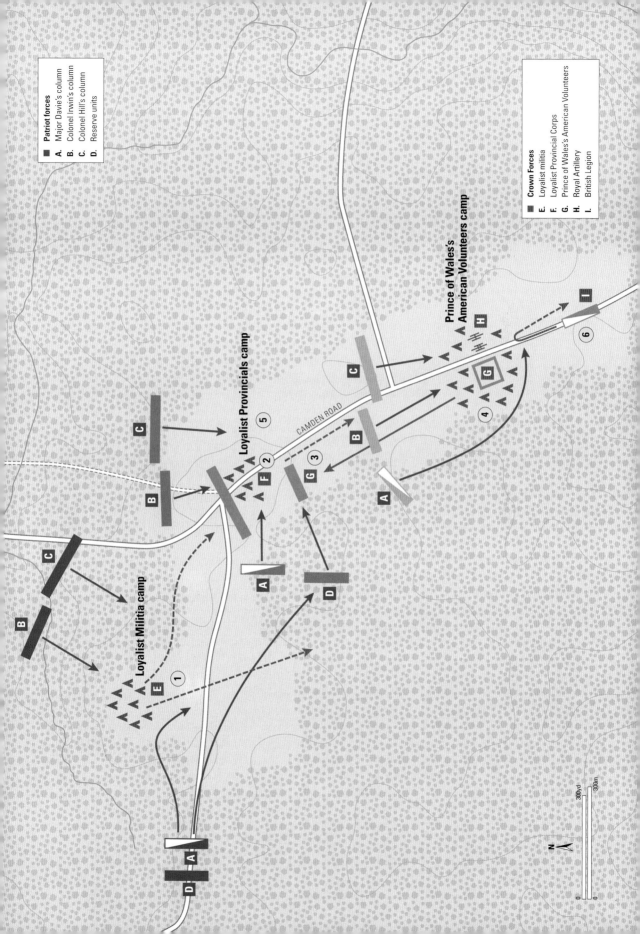

Patriot forces
■ A. Major Davie's column
  B. Colonel Irwin's column
  C. Colonel Hill's column
  D. Reserve units

Crown Forces
■ E. Loyalist militia
  F. Loyalist Provincial Corps
  G. Prince of Wales's American Volunteers
  H. Royal Artillery
  I. British Legion

Prince of Wales's
American Volunteers camp

Loyalist Provincials camp

CAMDEN ROAD

Loyalist Militia camp

N

300yd
300m

INTO COMBAT

The Patriot columns moved out at dawn on August 6, around 0615hrs. They had local guides, but it wasn't long before they ran into trouble. The main force left the road to avoid the pickets set around the most north-westerly encampment, housing the militia. The intention was to return to it using a defile near the camp to mask their approach, but Davie reported that "the guides, through ignorance or timidity, led them so far to the left, that the right and centre divisions, together with the left, fell upon the Tory [Loyalist militia] encampment" (Davie 1848: 26). Rather than strike the three camps simultaneously, the confusion of the guides meant that the three columns struck the Loyalist militia encampment at the same time from the northwest and northeast.

The surprise, at least, seems to have been maintained. The militia "were briskly attacked both in front and flank, and soon routed with great slaughter" (Davie 1848: 26). One of the attacking columns had passed through the gorge itself, and had to cross a creek and climb up the rocks there before reaching the enemy. The Loyalists broke and fled southeast, away from the multiple prongs of the Patriot attack and toward the second camp, where the Provincials of the Royal North Carolina Regiment and the light infantry of the British Legion were stationed.

The firing had alerted the remaining two Loyalist positions. The British Legion light infantry, supported by the Royal North Carolinians and possibly some militia, took position behind a fence in order to meet the Patriot attack as it swept on through the first, fallen encampment. "Colonel Sumpter [sic] directed the weight of his attack against the legion infantry, which resisted his efforts with great coolness and bravery," wrote the commander of the Legion, Lieutenant-Colonel Banastre Tarleton, who was not present at the fight (Tarleton 1787: 98). It is probably around this time that one of the British Legion's commanders, Captain McCullough, was mortally wounded.

The light infantry's resistance did not last. The oncoming Patriots forced them back. Davie writes that the British Legion "broke and mingled in the flight of the loyalists, yielding their camp without another struggle to the [Patriot] militia" (Davie 1848: 27).

At this point the Patriot assault might have carried over into the last of the three encampments, were it not for the efforts of a section of the Prince of Wales's American Volunteers. Hearing the battle drawing closer to their own encampment, a company worked their way onto the Patriot flank "by a bold and skilful manoeuvre" and occupied the woods overlooking the second encampment (Davie 1848: 27). There they delivered a deadly close-range salvo. This discharge, at around 50yd, again checked the Patriots momentarily. They responded by taking "instinctively to the trees and brush huts, and returned the fire with deadly effect" (Davie 1848: 27).

The Loyalists had bought enough time to form themselves in the last of the three encampments. At this point the commander of the outpost, Major Carden, was wounded or suffered some sort of mental collapse – sources differ. Either way, he surrendered leadership to Captain Rousselet of the British Legion. Likely wary that an attack might come from another direction, and wanting to provide a focal point for the scattered Loyalists to rally to,

This Loyalist of the Queen's Rangers is armed with a rifle. The Queen's Rangers, commanded for much of the American Revolutionary War by Lieutenant-Colonel John Graves Simcoe, included a dedicated rifle company, likely equipped with .62-caliber Pattern 1776 "contract" rifles. Visible in this case is the shortened jacket and the leather cap, though like the British Legion, the Queen's Rangers opted to keep green Provincial Corps uniforms rather than the British red. (Courtesy of Toronto Public Library)

Rousselet formed the Prince of Wales's American Volunteers and the other remaining Provincials and militia into a hollow square protected by their nearby artillery. Rarely employed during the American Revolutionary War, this tactical formation provided a degree of security for Rousselet's men and stabilized the situation, giving the Loyalists a chance to reorganize before a total rout ensued. Davie described how the Loyalists "now retreated hastily to their former position, and drew up in the centre of the cleared grounds, in the form of a hollow square" (Davie 1848: 27).

Hanging Rock

Here we see the heart of the southernmost Loyalist camp during the battle of Hanging Rock. Major Carden has panicked and given over command to Captain John Rousselet of the British Legion's light infantry. The Loyalist officer is desperately attempting to organize a defense of the Loyalist camp and avert a rout. With him is a confused mix of his own Legion infantry, the Prince of Wales' American Volunteers, and some Loyalist militiaman from the first encampment to have been attacked, farther north. At Rousselet's instruction the men are forming a hollow square, a last-ditch rally point for the camp's defenders. Beyond them the remains of fire pits and brush huts indicate where the camp has been overturned during the chaos of the surprise Patriot attack. The distant tree line is occupied by Patriot riflemen, but they are at the limit of their effective range, and cannot close it for fear of being exposed to nearby British artillery. Already, many of Sumter's men have chosen to loot the other two overrun Loyalist camps rather than attempt to destroy the defiant square.

During the desperate fighting, both sides showed the best of their abilities. Before being pushed back into the square the British Legion's light infantry fixed bayonets and counterattacked – Tarleton praised "the example of courage exhibited by one hundred and sixty men of the legion, who charged the Americans twice with fixed bayonets, to save their three pounder" (Tarleton 1787: 97). The defense of the artillery pieces in particular proved vital to allowing the Loyalists to hold on. On the other side, Sumter's riflemen commenced targeting the Loyalists at range over the course of a prolonged firefight. Davie recalled that "In a few minutes there was not a British officer standing" (Davie 1848: 27). This was an exaggeration, but casualties were indeed high among the Provincials who stood their ground. McCulloch, commanding the British Legion's light infantry, was mortally wounded during the fighting.

While the Patriot assault had driven the Loyalists back to their final encampment and pushed them to the brink of routing, their own attack was now almost spent. Sumter had his riflemen take to the trees flanking the third encampment and the hollow square planted at its center. From there they fired at the Loyalists, but the range meant that not enough Patriot firepower could be brought to bear to destroy the formation. Davie described how the riflemen "formed on the margin of the woods, and a heavy but ineffectual fire was commenced" (Davie 1848: 28). The riflemen were reluctant to close the range in the face of Loyalist return fire and the potential discharge of their artillery, which Davie reported kept up a continuous fire.

At one point a number of Loyalists earlier scattered by the Patriot attack were able to rally away from the square, on the edge of the woodland on the far side of the third encampment. A mixture of militia as well as Provincials and some of the British Legion's light infantry, these men "might take the Americans in flank" (Davie 1848: 28). Davie and his mounted detachment were sent to circumnavigate the firefight raging across the encampment's remains and, using the trees as cover, charged. "They were already dispirited under the impression of defeat," Davie wrote, "and were all routed and dispersed in a few minutes by this handful of men" (Davie 1848: 28).

Despite this Patriot success, the hollow square in the encampment's center seemed no closer to breaking: "The distance of the square from the woods, and the constant fire of two pieces of field-artillery, prevented the [Patriot] militia from making any considerable impression on the British troops" (Davie 1848: 28). To compound their difficulties further, ammunition began to run short for the Patriots. Sumter was reported to have "supplied himself by stripping it from the fallen and wounded tories" (quoted in James 1829: 90). Sumter later claimed that his inability completely to defeat the outpost was due to the lack of ammunition.

At this point Patriot discipline began to deteriorate rapidly. The indiscipline of which militiamen were sometimes accused reared its head, as instead of maintaining the pressure on the Loyalist square from the tree line, men began to ransack the two Crown Forces encampments that had already been overrun. The day was a hot one and, coupled with a discovery of a supply of rum, the potential for Patriot disaster was obvious. Davie lamented that "The commissary stores were taken in the centre camp, and numbers of the men were already intoxicated. The greater part were loaded with plunder, and those in a condition to fight had exhausted their ammunition" (Davie 1848: 29). Another Patriot partisan leader, Henry Lee, wrote that "the spoils of the camp, and the free use of spirits in which the enemy abounded, had for some time attracted and incapacitated our soldiers" (Lee 1812: 171). Only about 200 riflemen and Davie's small detachment of cavalry remained capable of continuing the fight.

With the Patriot attack having lost all momentum, Sumter chose to make the most of his successes so far before withdrawing. The Patriots finished "plundering the camp, taking the paroles of the British officers, and preparing litters for the wounded" (Davie 1848: 29). The hollow square maintained its ground, the men watching the activity of the enemy and "consoled themselves with some military music, and an interlude of three cheers for King George, which was immediately answered by three cheers for the hero of American liberty" (Davie 1848: 29).

Around this point the final act of the engagement took place. A detachment of 40 light infantrymen from the British Legion, mounted on horseback, were on their way from the neighboring outposts at Rocky Mount to Hanging Rock. Their commanders, Captain Patrick Stewart and Captain Charles McDonald, detected the sounds of battle at Hanging Rock and hastened with their small force "to reinforce their companions" (Tarleton 1787: 98). Taking a circuitous route to reach the main Camden road, they devised a ploy to attempt to make their command appear more formidable than it really was. The mounted light infantrymen were "ordered to extend their files, in order to look like a formidable detachment" (Tarleton 1787: 98). A bugle horn, usually sounded to give orders to the light infantry when they were dismounted, was instead "directed to sound the charge" while the men were still riding (Tarleton 1787: 98). The effect of all of this was to trick the Patriots into believing that a large force of British Legion dragoons had arrived and were charging to the rescue of the Loyalist encampment.

Just how effective the light infantry's *ruse de guerre* was remains a matter of dispute. Tarleton claimed that "this unexpected appearance deranged

A view of the muzzle and bayonet of a replica British musket of the American Revolutionary War period. Often described by modern-day sources as being only for fixing a bayonet rather than aiming, the nub near the muzzle was actually described as a sight in contemporary sources. Certainly, British light infantrymen seem to have been capable shots in combat. (Author's Collection)

the American commander, and threw his corps into a state of confusion, which produced a general retreat" (Tarleton 1787: 98). Another British Legion officer, Major George Hanger, also stated that "the approach of the detachment under Captains M'Donald and Stewart, &c. &c. as related by Colonel Tarleton, obliged General Sumpter to quit the field, and desist from any further attack on that post" (Hanger 1789: 30). While it appears the Patriots mistook the British Legion's light infantry for their dragoons, the impact of their sudden arrival was dismissed. Davie wrote that "some of the Legion cavalry appeared drawn up on the Camden road ... but on being charged by Davie's dragoons, they all took to the woods in flight, and one only was cut down" (Davie 1848: 29). Lee recorded "a party was now for the first time seen drawn up on the Cambden [sic] road, with the appearance of renewal of the contest; but on the approach of Davie it fell back (Lee 1812: 171). It does seem as though, regardless of the Loyalist reinforcements, the plundering of the encampments went on undisturbed, and Sumter was able to withdraw without further contest.

While small in terms of the numbers engaged, the battle of Hanging Rock had been a ferocious one, especially considering it only lasted half the day. While losses among the Loyalist militia were light due to many of them having fled at the beginning of the engagement, among the Provincials the Patriot riflemen had inflicted greater casualties. The British Legion had lost three officers, including McCulloch, and 20 men, with another 30 wounded – one-third of the light infantry stationed at the outpost. The Prince of Wales's American Volunteers also suffered heavily, sustaining over 100 casualties. The Patriots took 72 prisoners, including three officers. For their own part, at least according to Sumter, the Patriots suffered 20 dead, 40 wounded, and two missing. Lee reported that "our loss was not ascertained, from the usual inattention to returns prevalent with militia officers; and many of our wounded were immediately carried home from the field of battle" (Lee 1812: 171). Loyalist accuracy was seemingly not without merit either – among the Patriot casualties were an ensign, two lieutenants, a captain, a major, and a colonel, all wounded, and two captains were killed. Among their spoils the Patriots also counted 100 horses and 250 muskets, taken from the pillaged Loyalist encampments.

Tactically, Sumter's attack on Hanging Rock had failed. The British garrison narrowly avoided being overrun. The Patriot militia were forced to withdraw. They did so, however, having ransacked most of the garrison's encampment, including seizing weapons and supplies, and likely inflicted over twice the number of casualties they suffered. There were even claims that the Prince of Wales's American Volunteers largely ceased to exist after the battle. While this was an exaggeration (elements of the regiment served in several more engagements), Loyalist morale was shaken by the attack, while Sumter's militia continued to undermine Crown authority with their raids. Hanging Rock was reinforced for a while by British regulars, drawing them from vital duties elsewhere. Tarleton admitted that Sumter's check at Hanging Rock "did not discourage him, or injure his cause: The loss of men was easily supplied, and his reputation for activity and courage was fully established by his late enterprizing conduct" (Tarleton 1787: 98).

Analysis

The engagements at Harlem Heights, Freeman's Farm, and Hanging Rock all emphasized the strengths and limitations of both the British light infantry and the Patriot riflemen who opposed them. In all three engagements the Patriot riflemen exacted a toll on their Crown Forces foes, initially driving them back. The deadly marksmanship of Morgan's corps in particular was noted at Freeman's Farm, where a large number of officers as well as artillery crewmen were casualties. At Harlem Heights and Hanging Rock the usefulness of the rifle's ranged superiority seems a little less pronounced, though the British were forced to give up the ground at Harlem Heights and their light infantry were driven back in retreat for the first time since Lexington and Concord. The rifle did not seem to dominate exclusively in firefights, however. In all three engagements the riflemen themselves suffered losses, including among

A late-19th-century view of where the Jones farmhouse – the scene of fighting at the start and possibly the end of the battle of Harlem Heights – once stood. It occupied the slightly raised ground in the center of the picture. (Classic Collection 3/Alamy Stock Photo)

their officers, and failed to deliver a decisive knockout blow during prolonged ranged encounters. Light infantry seem to have been capable of holding their own in a contest of marksmanship with some riflemen, if not the most elite. At Throg's Neck on October 18, 1776, for example, British light infantry engaged in an extended firefight with Patriot riflemen and overcame them at range.

The vulnerability of riflemen during close-quarters combat was also evident in two of the three engagements. Only at Harlem Heights, where they cooperated closely with bayonet-armed infantry, were the Patriot riflemen not driven back by a light-infantry charge at some point during the engagement. At Freeman's Farm, between their initial success and their effectiveness in a supporting role later in the day, the riflemen were routed after failing to coordinate properly with their bayonet-equipped support. At Hanging Rock, the riflemen were initially stymied by a bayonet charge and refused to close the distance with the remnants of the last Loyalist encampment, thereby missing out on the opportunity to secure a total Patriot victory. Conversely, the bayonet charges made by the Loyalist light infantry at Hanging Rock secured their artillery and bought time for friendly troops to rally, helping to stem the possibility of a Crown Forces rout. The difficulty riflemen experienced when it came to taking ground again emphasized that their effectiveness only really translated into wider battlefield success when they were used alongside bayonet-armed infantry.

In all three engagements the British light infantry exhibited good discipline and morale, though the fact that they were checked and ultimately driven back at Harlem Heights appears to have taken the edge off the overconfidence they often displayed. By contrast, the Patriot riflemen's discipline during combat proved to be a mixed bag. At Freeman's Farm, despite his men being badly scattered after their initial charge, Morgan was able to effectively rally them and provide a vital contribution during the battle – testimony to the fact that his corps was probably the best force of riflemen available to Washington during the American Revolutionary War. On the other hand, Sumter's inability to finish off Loyalist forces at Hanging Rock owed much to the fact that many of his men preferred to loot the captured Crown Forces encampments and seize the rum supply rather than close with the wavering enemy. This contrast can be readily explained by the fact that Morgan's corps was composed of experienced Continental Army regulars, while the men under Sumter's command, despite including some veterans, were essentially a militia force uncomfortable with full military discipline. Such a difference highlights the difficulties faced by Continental commanders when trying to assign roles to rifle units, whose performance in action could vary considerably, and also explains why some officers highlighted the effectiveness of riflemen while others despaired at their failings. Inconsistency did much to undermine the prestige initially accorded the rifle among Patriot forces.

The availability of light infantrymen versus riflemen also had an important impact on their tactical uses. As Tarleton suggested and Washington complained, Patriot forces usually had an excess of riflemen that meant that losses were easily replaced. Even major British victories that resulted in the death or capture of hundreds of Patriot riflemen, as at Long Island, did not dent the numbers available to Patriot forces. It was often more a case of finding the riflemen

This plaque commemorating the battle of Harlem Heights shows hunting shirt-clad riflemen as well as a fallen Patriot officer. Given the wounded figure is likewise in a hunting shirt, it may well represent Major Andrew Leitch, who was hit by three separate musket balls while leading his Virginian riflemen during the action, and died 12 days later. (Library of Congress)

TO COMMEMORATE THE BATTLE OF HARLEM HEIGHTS, WON BY
WASHINGTON'S TROOPS ON THIS SITE, SEPTEMBER 16, 1776.
ERECTED BY THE SONS OF THE REVOLUTION IN THE STATE OF NEW YORK

duties that could effectively utilize their strengths while mitigating their stark weaknesses. By contrast, there were never enough light infantrymen to fulfil the tasks British commanders wished to undertake. As the experienced elite of an army that was already undersized and often outnumbered, the light infantry was a prime force called upon to carry out all manner of roles and operations, from scouting to screening and from foraging to acting as shock troops on the battlefield. The attrition among light infantry throughout the American Revolutionary War was intense, with some companies suffering two or three times their initial number in losses, relying on a constant stream of drafts to replace casualties. The composite flank battalions were simply irreplaceable, hence Burgoyne's reluctance to employ them fully at Freeman's Farm, where their use would likely have softened the heavy impact on the British line regiments engaged. Even minor losses could be debilitating not only to the light battalions but subsequently to the army as a whole, as replacements had to be brought in from the regular battalion companies to maintain the flank companies at full strength. This bias toward light infantry and grenadiers contributed to the draining of the line regiments. Simply put, the sheer manpower of Patriot riflemen was far superior to that fielded as British light infantry, and the predisposition of the British toward aggressive tactics even when outnumbered only exposed them to the danger of further losses.

Aftermath

Dating from 1790, shortly before the British Army became involved in another prolonged conflict, the French Revolutionary Wars (1792–1802), this illustration depicts two soldiers of a British Army center company – "hat men" – alongside a light infantryman. This difference in headgear and uniform between different companies of the same regiment would persist until the issue of a short-tailed jacket and "stovepipe" shako to all other ranks of the British Army's infantry in 1800, with infantry officers also dispensing with long-tailed coats and cocked hats in 1812. The light infantry and grenadiers operated closely together throughout the American Revolutionary War and developed a close rapport, with grenadiers typically referring to the light infantry as their "children." (Anne S.K. Brown Military Collection, Brown University Library)

While Patriot riflemen proved challenging adversaries, the British Army responded well to the threat they posed. It seems that for the most part British light infantry quickly overcome any initial fear that Patriot riflemen induced, and became effective at countering them. Captain William Dansey of the 33rd Foot's light company reported bettering riflemen at Long Island, Throg's Neck, and Ash Swamp on June 24, 1777, boasting that being armed with a rifle alone did not make a marksman and that a well-trained regular soldier was sure of bettering them despite their fearsome reputation (Dansey 2010:

14–24). British light infantry were well employed engaging and neutralizing enemy riflemen, not only by engaging the enemy at close quarters, but also often by matching them at range. This only changed noticeably when the riflemen in question were among the better companies fielded by the Patriots.

For example, some months after Hanging Rock, Sumter's militia encircled an isolated party of 20 Loyalist light infantrymen from the Provincial Corps. Despite being surrounded and hugely outnumbered, the light infantry again formed a hollow square and kept up such an intensity of fire that the militia were unable to overwhelm them. When called on to surrender, they displayed typical light-infantry elan by declaring that light infantry never surrender. Certainly, instances of light infantry being comprehensively bettered by riflemen seem to have been extremely rare.

One of the greatest benefits provided by American riflemen to the Patriot cause was from the perspective of morale. The use of rifles by Americans, especially American frontiersmen, was well known to the British Army and the British public in general. Officers not yet acquainted with the realities of fighting in America feared the rifle's range and accuracy. British forces suffered losses to opportune sniping and the targeting of pickets and sentries by marksmen. While these casualties were minor, they at times had a debilitating effect on the British Army's spirit. Riflemen also helped lift the morale of Patriot soldiers and civilians, especially during the crucial early months of the American Revolutionary War. Fellow revolutionaries viewed them as hardy frontiersmen and expert shots who could be relied upon to advance the cause of liberty and reap a heavy toll on the British. In reality this was rarely the case, but the initial perception was important, and valuable.

The actual combat effectiveness of Patriot riflemen is difficult to quantify, given that it varied considerably from unit to unit and from one theater of the war to another. During the campaigns of 1775 to 1779 the rifle played a steadily diminishing role, with the effectiveness of Morgan's corps at Saratoga a definite high point. Ultimately, the rifle's origins as a hunting weapon and not a weapon of war undermined its effectiveness, and Continental Army officers were generally happy to phase it out of service. One officer, Colonel Peter Muhlenberg, complained about how difficult rifles were to maintain in wartime conditions, writing that "on a march, where soldiers are without tents, and their arms continually exposed to the weather, rifles are of little use. I would therefore request your Excellency to convert my regiment into musketry" (Muhlenberg 1849: 74). Washington's aide-de-camp, Lieutenant Colonel George Johnston, replied on the general's behalf, writing that Washington agreed with Muhlenberg's concerns and had decided that as few rifles as possible were to be used – he would replace the weapons with muskets. This process was repeated throughout the American Revolutionary War.

Even so, the rifle proved perhaps most effective not in the hard campaigning in the North with Washington's main army, but during the British efforts to subdue the South from 1780 onward. Small-scale fighting and irregular warfare – conducted by both sides – emphasized the rifle's strengths. At Kings Mountain, a force of 1,000 riflemen won one of the foremost Patriot victories of the American Revolutionary War. At both

A 1798 cartoon of William Pitt the Younger, British prime minister for much of the period between 1783 and his death in 1806. Immediately recognizable, light-infantry headgear and uniforms featured prominently in satirical depictions of British politicians and soldiers in the French Revolutionary Wars. This caricature gives the Tory statesman a crested helmet and short-tailed coat of the style that continued to be associated with light infantrymen in the decades after the British Army's defeat in North America. (Anne S.K. Brown Military Collection, Brown University Library)

A 1905 depiction of the battle of Fallen Timbers on August 20, 1794, the final battle of the Northwest Indian War (1786–95). The Kentucky militia involved at Fallen Timbers, the first victory of the nascent US Army, were likely armed with a mixture of rifled and smoothbore firearms. (Universal History Archive/Universal Images Group via Getty Images)

Cowpens on January 17, 1781, and Guilford Courthouse, riflemen were also used to good effect in the opening stages of the fighting, combining well with smoothbore-armed regular infantry. While still not the weapon that some Patriots in 1775 had thought would win them the American Revolutionary War, the rifle caused additional casualties that the British, especially in the South, could ill-afford. British light infantry especially were lacking in that theater, with the composite battalions not deployed until 1781.

Some Patriot commanders continued to appreciate the rifle's usefulness, however. Its ability to extend the range of combat and supplement firepower combined with the numerical advantage often enjoyed by Patriot forces to ensure that they remained superior during firefights for most of the American Revolutionary War. Major General Lafayette wrote after one action in 1777: "I found the riflemen above even their reputation" (Lafayette 1837: 122). In 1781, before marching to Yorktown, Washington found himself lamenting the fact that he now had too few riflemen, as many had been deployed to the western or southern theaters or replaced by smoothbore-armed troops.

Overall, British light infantry were a crucial part of efforts to engage the Patriots on their own ground and in their own style of fighting. The Patriots were able to replace their losses, however, while the small cadre of light infantry available to the British was unable to cope with the American Revolutionary War's intensity and the demands placed upon them by increasingly desperate Crown Forces commanders. The Patriots were also able successfully to copy the light-infantry model used by the British regulars. Ultimately, Washington preferred light infantry armed with smoothbore muskets and bayonets over the rifle companies that had been organized at the start of the American Revolutionary War. While riflemen were rarely as effective as many modern sources make out, their contribution to the Patriot cause was far from negligible.

UNIT ORGANIZATIONS

Patriot

At first, the newly raised Patriot rifle companies generally managed to achieve their relatively large establishment strength, which included one captain, three lieutenants, four sergeants, four corporals, one musician, and 68 privates. Over the next two years, however, many of these units were amalgamated with others or disbanded, the remainder being joined by successive waves of rifle companies and regiments raised for the Continental Army, the State forces, and among the militia. Many of these had different company strengths. For example, Captain John Nelson's Independent Rifle Company, raised in 1776 in the Pennsylvanian backcountry for service on the frontier and in Canada, consisted of one captain, three lieutenants, four sergeants, four corporals, and 70 privates. Meanwhile, the rifle companies raised as part of the Virginian regiments of the Continental Army – some of which saw action at the battle of Harlem Heights – each fielded one captain, two lieutenants, one ensign, three sergeants, two musicians (one drummer and one fifer), and 68 privates.

The Continental Army also underwent almost yearly reorganizations that further muddied the waters in terms of establishment strength, and like their opponents suffered severe losses on campaign. Many Continental Army regiments engaged at the battle of Brandywine, for example, numbered only around 200 men, or even fewer, meaning individual company strength was correspondingly lower.

British

The size of British Army light-infantry companies varied a great deal throughout the American Revolutionary War, both in terms of official establishment and actual combat strength. In 1775, the official composition was one captain, two lieutenants, three sergeants, three corporals, one musician, and 36 privates. At the start of the conflict the British Army attempted to augment its forces by increasing the number of privates and drummers in each company. Units struggled to put these changes into effect immediately, however, and for the first year or so of the American Revolutionary War companies tended to hover around the prewar establishment numbers.

The British were able to push toward a larger establishment by 1777, whereby companies nominally consisted of one captain, two lieutenants, three sergeants, three corporals, two musicians, and 54 privates. Variations in actual unit strengths were compounded by losses on campaign, meaning companies were often considerably smaller than they should have been on paper. The companies of the 33rd Foot, for example, averaged fewer than 30 men each, all ranks, at the battle of Camden on August 16, 1780. Manpower shortages were felt particularly keenly by the British light companies, as their hard service led to a higher casualty ratio than any other force besides the grenadiers, requiring replacements frequently to be drawn from the regular battalion companies and thus further draining those companies of manpower and expertise.

George Washington welcoming the rifle companies to his camp during the siege of Boston, which commenced on April 19, 1775, and lasted until March 17, 1776, when the British evacuated their forces from the area. At this time early in the war the rifle companies were quite large, and on occasion there were actually too many riflemen with the Continental Army for effective use, but the vagaries of campaigning meant that numbers could fluctuate substantially. (GRANGER - Historicall Picture Archive/Alamy Stock Photo)

BIBLIOGRAPHY

Adams, John (1917). "Phyladelphia, June [July] 6th, 1775" in *Warren-Adams Letters, being chiefly a correspondence among John Adams, Samuel Adams, and James Warren, Vol. I*. Boston, MA: The Massachusetts Historical Society.

André, John, ed. Henry Cabot Lodge (1903). *André's journal: an authentic record of the movements and engagements of the British Army in America from June 1777 to November 1778 as recorded from day to day by Major John André*. Boston, MA: Bibliophile Society.

Baxter, James Phinney (1887). *The British Invasion from the North: The Campaigns of Generals Carleton and Burgoyne from Canada, 1776–1777*. Albany, NY: Joel Munsell's Sons.

Burgoyne, John (1780). *A State of the Expedition from Canada*. London: J. Almon.

Coote, Eyre, trans. Paul L. Pace (2011), "37th Light Infantry Company Order Book, 1778–1781." Available at http://www.revwar75.com/library/pace/37-light-OB.pdf

Cuthbertson, Bennett (1776). *Cuthbertson's System, for the Complete Interior Management and Œconomy of a Battalion of Infantry*. Bristol: Rouths & Nelson.

Dansey, William (2010). "Newport Rhode Island Jany 10th 1777," in Paul Dansey, ed., *Captured Rebel Flag: The Letters of Captain William Dansey, 33rd Regiment of Foot, 1776–1777*. Godmanchester: Ken Trotman Publishing.

Davie, William (1848). "Life of William Richardson Davie," in Jared Sparks, ed., *The Library of American Biography, Second Series, Vol. XV*. Boston, MA: Charles C. Little & James Brown.

Dearborn, Henry (1939). *Revolutionary War Journals of Henry Dearborn, 1775–1783*, eds. Lloyd A. Brown & Howard H. Peckham. Chicago, IL: The Caxton Club.

Evensen, Bruce J. (2018). *Journalism and the American Experience*. New York, NY: Routledge.

Force, Peter (1840). "Extract of a Letter to a Gentleman in Philadelphia, Dated Fredericktown, MD., August 1, 1775" in *American Archives: Fourth Series, Volume III*. Washington, DC: M. St. Clair Clarke & Peter Force.

Frost, John (1848). *Remarkable Events in the History of America from the Earliest Times to the Year 1848, Vol. II*. Philadelphia, PA: G.B. Zieber & Co.

Graham, James (1856). *The Life of General Daniel Morgan, of the Virginia Line of the Army of the United States*. New York, NY: Derby & Jackson.

Graham, William A. (1904). *General Joseph Graham and His Papers on North Carolina Revolutionary History*. Raleigh, NC: Edwards & Broughton.

Hanger, George (1789). *An Address to the Army; in reply to Strictures, by R. M'Kenzie*. London: James Ridgway.

Howe, William (1897). "Howe's Orders, dated Newtown, L.I., Sept. 13th," in Henry P. Johnston, ed., *The Battle of Harlem Heights, September 16, 1776*. New York, NY: The Columbia University Press.

Hubner, Brian (1986). *The Formation of the British Light Infantry Companies and their Employment in the Saratoga Campaign of 1777*. Saskatoon: University of Saskatchewan.

Hunter, Martin (1894). *The Journal of Gen. Sir Martin Hunter, G.C.M.G., G.C.H.: and some letters of his wife, Lady Hunter*. Edinburgh: Edinburgh Press.

James, William Dobein (1829). "Battle of Hanging Rock," in Theodore Burling, ed., *The Cabinet of Instruction, Literature and Amusement, Vol. I*. New York, NY: Theodore Burling.

Johnston, Henry Phelps. (1878). *The Campaign of 1776 around New York and Brooklyn*. Brooklyn, NY: Long Island Historical Society.

Johnston, Henry Phelps (1897). *Battle of Harlem Heights, September 16, 1776*. New York, NY: Columbia University Press.

Ketchum, Richard M. (1997). *Saratoga: Turning Point of America's Revolutionary War*. New York, NY: Henry Holt & Co.

Knox, Henry (1873). "Camp Middlebrook, 21 June, 1777," in Francis S. Drake, ed., *Life and Correspondence of Henry Knox*. Boston, MA: Samuel G. Drake.

Lafayette, Gilbert du Motier (1837). *Memoirs, Correspondence and Manuscripts of General Lafayette, Vol. I*. London: Saunders & Otley.

Lamb, Roger (1809). *An Original and Authentic Journal of Occurrences during the Late American War*. Dublin: Wilkinson & Courtney.

Lee, Charles (1853). "Charleston, 21 June, 1776," in Jared Sparks, ed., *Correspondence of the American Revolution Vol. II*. Boston, MA: Little, Brown, & Co.

Lee, Henry (1812). *Memoirs of the War in the Southern Department of the United States, Vol. I*. Philadelphia, PA: Bradford & Inskeep.

Lee, Richard Henry (1859). "Feb. 24th, 1775," in John R. Thompson, ed., *The Southern Literary Messenger, Vol. 28*. Richmond, VA: MacFarlane, Fergusson & Co.

Lowell, Edward J. (1884). *The Hessians and the other German Auxiliaries of Great Britain in the Revolutionary War*. New York, NY: Harper & Bros.

Mackenzie, Frederick (1930). *The Diary of Frederick Mackenzie*. Cambridge, MA: Harvard University Press.

McGuire, Thomas J. (2000). *Paoli: The Revolutionary War "Massacre" Near Philadelphia*. Mechanicsburg, PA: Stackpole Books.

Moore, Frank (1856). *Songs and Ballads of the American Revolution*. New York, NY: D. Appleton & Company.

Moore, Frank (1876). *The Diary of the Revolution*. Hartford, CT: J.B. Burr Publishing Co.

Muhlenberg, Henry A. (1849). *The Life of Major-General Peter Muhlenberg of the Revolutionary Army*. Philadelphia, PA: Carey & Hart.

Nelson, Paul David (2005). *Francis Rawdon-Hastings, Marquess of Hastings: Soldier, Peer of the Realm, Governor-General of India*. Madison, NJ: Fairleigh Dickinson University Press.

Peters, Richard (1893). "War Office October 26th 1776," in William Hand Browne, ed., *Archives of Maryland: Journal and Correspondence of the Maryland Council of Safety, July 7–December 31, 1776*. Baltimore, MD: Maryland Historical Society.

Scribner, Robert L. (1973). *Revolutionary Virginia, the Road to Independence: The Committee of Safety and the Balance of Forces, 1775*. Charlottesville, VA: University of Virginia Press.

Simes, Thomas (1768). *The Military Medley: Containing the most necessary rules and directions for attaining a competent knowledge of the art*. London: publisher not known.

Snow, Dean (2016). *1777: Tipping Point at Saratoga*. Oxford: Oxford University Press.

Spring, Matthew (2008). *With Zeal and With Bayonets Only: The British Army on Campaign in North America, 1775–1783*. Norman, OK: University of Oklahoma Press.

Stone, William L. (1891). *Letters of Braunschweig and Hessian Officers during the American Revolution*. Albany, NY: Joel Munsell's Sons.

Tarleton, Banastre (1787). *A History of the Campaigns of 1780 and 1781 In the Southern Provinces of North America*. Dublin: Colles, Exshaw, White, H. Whitestone, Burton, Byrne, Moore, Jones & Dornin.

Thatcher, James (1823). *A Military Journal during the American Revolutionary War*. Boston, MA: Richardson & Lord.

Thomas, John (1883). "Oct. 24 1775," in George W. Williams, ed., *History of the Negro Race in America from 1619 to 1880, Volume I*. New York, NY: G.P. Putnam's Sons.

Townshend, George (1894). "Rules and Orders for the Discipline of the Light Infantry Companies in His Majesty's Army in Ireland," in Raymond Henry Raymond Smythies, ed., *Historical Records of the 40th (2nd Somersetshire) Regiment*. Devonport: A.H. Smith.

Urwin, Gregory J.W. (2019). "'To bring the American Army under strict Discipline': British Army Foraging Policy in the South, 1780–81," *War in History*, 26(1): 11.

Wakefield, Ezekie (1880). "Unpublished Recollections of the Campaign of 1777," in *The United Service: A Monthly Review of Military and Naval Affairs, Vol. III*. Philadelphia, PA: L.R. Hamersly & Co.

Washington, George (1796). *Official Letters to the Honourable American Congress Vol. I*. Boston, MA: Manning & Loring.

Washington, George (1881). *Proceedings of the American Antiquarian Society, Vol. 1*. Worcester, MA: Press of Chas. Hamilton.

Washington, George (1933). *The Writings of George Washington from the Original Manuscript Sources 1745–1799, Vol. 8*. Washington, DC: Government Printing Office.

Washington, George (1939). *The Writings of George Washington from the Original Manuscript Sources 1745–1799, Vol. 9*. Washington, DC: Government Printing Office.

Wayne, Anthony (1893). "Mount Joy 8th Feby 1778," in Charles J. Stille, ed., *Major-General Anthony Wayne and the Pennsylvania Line in the Continental Army*. Philadelphia, PA: J.B. Lippincott Company.

Wilkinson, James (1816). *Memoirs of My Own Times, Vol. I*. Philadelphia, PA: Abraham Small.

Wright, John W. (1924). "The Rifle in the American Revolution," *The American Historical Review* 29.2: 293–99.

INDEX